Microsoft® Office PowerPoint® 2010

Level 1

Microsoft® Office PowerPoint® 2010: Level 1

Part Number: 084592
Course Edition: 1.1

NOTICES

What is the Microsoft Office Specialist Certification Program?

The Microsoft Office Specialist (MOS) Certification Program enables candidates to show that they have something exceptional to offer - proven expertise in Microsoft® Office programs. The MOS Certification Program is the only Microsoft-approved certification program of its kind. The MOS Certification exams focus on validating specific skill sets within each of the Microsoft® Office system programs. The candidate can choose which exam(s) they want to take according to which skills they want to validate. The available MOS exams include:

- MOS: Microsoft® Office Word 2010
- MOS: Microsoft® Office Excel 2010
- MOS: Microsoft® Office PowerPoint 2010
- MOS: Microsoft® Office Outlook 2010
- MOS: Microsoft® Office Access 2010
- MOS: Microsoft® SharePoint 2010

For more information:

Your comments are important to us. Please contact us at Element K Press LLC, 1-800-478-7788, 500 Canal View Boulevard, Rochester, NY 14623, Attention: Product Planning, or through our Web site at **http://support.elementkcourseware.com.**

To learn more about MOS exams, visit **www.microsoft.com/learning/en/us/certification/mos.aspx**.

To learn about other MOS approved courseware from Element K, visit **www.elementkcourseware.com**

* The availability of Microsoft Certified exams varies by Microsoft Office program, program version and language. Visit **www.microsoft.com/learning/en/us/default.aspx** for exam availability.

Microsoft, the Office Logo, Outlook, and PowerPoint are either registered trademarks or trademarks of Microsoft Corporation in the United States and/or other countries. The MOS Logos are used under license from Microsoft Corporation.

Microsoft® Office PowerPoint® 2010: Level 1

About This Course

In today's work environment, presentations have moved far beyond flip charts and overhead projectors. Audiences not only expect presentations to be in the electronic format, but also demand them to be unique and use interactive elements to keep them engaged. In this course, you will use Microsoft® Office PowerPoint® 2010 to create presentations.

Using PowerPoint to create and deliver presentations will capture the attention of the audience and will help communicate the ideas of the presenter more effectively. PowerPoint 2010 possesses advanced design features, enhanced illustrations, and graphical elements that make presentation creation as well as viewing a truly delightful experience.

Course Description

Target Student

This course is designed for students who are interested in learning the fundamentals needed to create and modify basic presentations using Microsoft Office PowerPoint 2010.

Course Prerequisites

Students should be familiar with using personal computers, and have used a mouse and keyboard. They should be comfortable with the Windows environment and be able to use Windows to manage information on their computers. Specifically, they should be able to launch and close programs; navigate to information stored on the computer; and manage files and folders. Students should have completed the following courses or possess equivalent knowledge before starting with this course:

- Microsoft® Office Windows® XP Introduction
- Microsoft® Office Windows® XP Professional Level 1
- Microsoft® Office Windows® XP Professional Level 2
- Microsoft® Office Windows® 2000 Introduction

Course Objectives

In this course, you will explore the PowerPoint environment and create a presentation. You will format text on slides to enhance clarity. To enhance the visual appeal, you will add graphical objects to a presentation and modify them. You will also add tables and charts to a presentation to present data in a structured form. You will then finalize a presentation to deliver it.

You will:

- Identify the components of the PowerPoint 2010 interface.
- Create a basic presentation.
- Format text on slides.
- Add graphical objects to a presentation.
- Modify graphical objects in a presentation.
- Work with tables in a presentation.
- Add charts to a presentation.
- Prepare to deliver a presentation.

Certification

This course is designed to help you prepare for the following certification.

Certification Path: MOS: Microsoft Office PowerPoint 2010

This course is one of a series of Element K courseware titles that addresses Microsoft Office Specialist (MOS) certification skill sets. The MOS certification program is for individuals who use Microsoft's business desktop software and who seek recognition for their expertise with specific Microsoft products.

How to Use This Book

As a Learning Guide

This book is divided into lessons and topics, covering a subject or a set of related subjects. In most cases, lessons are arranged in order of increasing proficiency. The results-oriented topics include relevant and supporting information you need to master the content. Each topic has various types of activities designed to enable you to practice the guidelines and procedures as well as to solidify your understanding of the informational material presented in thc course. At the back of the book, you will find a glossary of the definitions of the terms and concepts used throughout the course. You will also find an index to assist in locating information within the instructional components of the book.

In the Classroom

This book is intended to enhance and support the in-class experience. Procedures and guidelines are presented in a concise fashion along with activities and discussions. Information is provided for reference and reflection in such a way as to facilitate understanding and practice.

Each lesson may also include a Lesson Lab or various types of simulated activities. You will find the files for the simulated activities along with the other course files on the enclosed CD-ROM. If your course manual did not come with a CD-ROM, please go to **http:// elementkcourseware.com** to download the files. If included, these interactive activities enable you to practice your skills in an immersive business environment, or to use hardware and software resources not available in the classroom. The course files that are available on the CD-ROM or by download may also contain sample files, support files, and additional reference materials for use both during and after the course.

As a Teaching Guide

Effective presentation of the information and skills contained in this book requires adequate preparation. As such, as an instructor, you should familiarize yourself with the content of the entire course, including its organization and approaches. You should review each of the student activities and exercises so you can facilitate them in the classroom.

Throughout the book, you may see Instructor Notes that provide suggestions, answers to problems, and supplemental information for you, the instructor. You may also see references to "Additional Instructor Notes" that contain expanded instructional information; these notes appear in a separate section at the back of the book. PowerPoint slides may be provided on the included course files, which are available on the enclosed CD-ROM or by download from **http://www.elementk.com/courseware-file-downloads**. The slides are also referred to in the text. If you plan to use the slides, it is recommended to display them during the corresponding content as indicated in the instructor notes in the margin.

The course files may also include assessments for the course, which can be administered diagnostically before the class, or as a review after the course is completed. These exam-type questions can be used to gauge the students' understanding and assimilation of course content.

As a Review Tool

Any method of instruction is only as effective as the time and effort you, the student, are willing to invest in it. In addition, some of the information that you learn in class may not be important to you immediately, but it may become important later. For this reason, we encourage you to spend some time reviewing the content of the course after your time in the classroom.

As a Reference

The organization and layout of the book make it easy to use as a learning tool and as an after-class reference. You can use this book as a first source for definitions of terms, background information on given topics, and summaries of procedures.

Course Icons

Icon	Description
	A **Caution Note** makes students aware of potential negative consequences of an action, setting, or decision that are not easily known.
	Display Slide provides a prompt to the instructor to display a specific slide. Display Slides are included in the Instructor Guide only.
	An **Instructor Note** is a comment to the instructor regarding delivery, classroom strategy, classroom tools, exceptions, and other special considerations. Instructor Notes are included in the Instructor Guide only.
	Notes Page indicates a page that has been left intentionally blank for students to write on.
	A **Student Note** provides additional information, guidance, or hints about a topic or task.
	A **Version Note** indicates information necessary for a specific version of software.

Course Requirements

Hardware

For this course, you will need one computer for each student and one for the instructor. Each computer will need the following minimum hardware configurations:

- 1 GHz Pentium-class processor or faster
- Minimum 256 MB of RAM (512 MB of RAM recommended)
- 10 GB hard disk or larger (You should have at least 1 GB of free hard disk space available for the Office installation.)
- CD-ROM drive
- Keyboard and mouse or other pointing device
- 1024 x 768 resolution monitor recommended
- Network cards and cabling for local network access
- Internet access (contact your local network administrator)
- Printer (optional) or an installed printer driver
- Projection system to display the instructor's computer screen

Software

- Microsoft® Office Professional Edition 2010
- Microsoft® Office Suite Service Pack 1

● Microsoft® Windows® XP Professional with Service Pack 2

Class Setup

For Initial Class Setup

1. Install Windows XP Professional on an empty partition.

    ■ Leave the Administrator password blank.

    ■ For all other installation parameters, use values that are appropriate for your environment (see your local network administrator for details).

2. On Windows XP Professional, disable the **Welcome** screen. (This step ensures that students will be able to log on as the Administrator user regardless of what other user accounts exist on the computer.)

    a. Click **Start** and choose **Control Panel→User Accounts.**

    b. Click **Change The Way Users Log On And Off.**

    c. Uncheck **Use Welcome Screen.**

    d. Click **Apply Options.**

3. On Windows XP Professional, install Service Pack 2. Use the Service Pack installation defaults.

4. On the computer, install a printer driver (a physical print device is optional). Click **Start** and choose **Printers and Faxes.** Under **Printer Tasks,** click **Add a Printer** and follow the prompts.

    If you do not have a physical printer installed, right-click the printer and choose **Pause Printing** to prevent any print error message.

5. Run the **Internet Connection Wizard** to set up the Internet connection as appropriate for your environment, if you did not do so during installation.

6. Display known file type extensions.

    a. Right-click **Start** and select **Explore** to open Windows Explorer.

    b. Choose **Tools→Folder Options.**

    c. On the **View** tab, in the **Advanced Settings** list box, uncheck **Hide Extensions For Known File Types.**

    d. Click **Apply** and then click **OK.**

    e. Close Windows Explorer.

7. Log on to the computer as the Administrator user if you have not already done so.

8. Perform a complete installation of Microsoft Office Professional 2007.

9. In the **User Name** dialog box, click **OK** to accept the default user name and initials.

10. In the **Microsoft Office 2010 Activation Wizard** dialog box, click **Next** to activate the Office 2010 application.

11. When the activation of Microsoft Office 2010 is complete, click **Close** to close the **Microsoft Office 2010 Activation Wizard** dialog box.

12. In the **User Name** dialog box, click **OK.**

13. In the **Welcome To Microsoft 2010** dialog box, click **Finish.** You must have an active Internet connection to complete this step. Here, you select the **Download and Install Updates From Microsoft Update When Available (Recommended)** option, so that whenever there is a new update, it gets automatically installed on your system.

14. After the Microsoft Update runs, in the **Microsoft Office** dialog box, click **OK.**

15. Minimize the language bar, if necessary.

16. On the course CD-ROM, open the 084_592 folder. Then, open the Data folder. Run the 084592dd.exe self-extracting file located within. This will install a folder named 084592Data on your C drive. This folder contains all the data files you will use to complete this course.

   Within each lesson folder, you may find a Solution folder. This folder contains solution files for the lesson's activities and lesson lab, which can be used by students to check their end results.

Customize the Windows Desktop

Customize the Windows desktop to display the **My Computer** and **My Network Places** icons on the student and instructor systems by following the steps mentioned below.

1. Right-click the desktop and choose **Properties.**

2. Select the **Desktop** tab.

3. Click **Customize Desktop.**

4. In the **Desktop Items** dialog box, check the **My Computer** and **My Network Places** check boxes.

5. Click **OK** and click **Apply.**

6. Close the **Display Properties** dialog box.

Before Every Class

1. Log on to the computer as the Administrator user.

2. Delete any existing data file from the C:\084592Data folder.

3. Extract a fresh copy of the course data files from the CD-ROM provided with the course manual.

List of Additional Files

Printed with each activity is a list of files students open to complete that activity. Many activities also require additional files that students do not open, but are needed to support the file(s) students are working with. These supporting files are included with the student data files on the course CD-ROM or data disk. Do not delete these files.

1 Getting Started with PowerPoint

Lesson Time: 45 minutes

Lesson Objectives:

In this lesson, you will identify the components of the PowerPoint 2010 interface.

You will:

● Identify the elements of the user interface.

● View presentations.

● Save a presentation.

● Use Microsoft PowerPoint Help.

Introduction

Using PowerPoint, you can create dynamic presentations to captivate the attention of the audience, as well as communicate difficult concepts clearly and effectively. Familiarizing yourself with the PowerPoint application and the various options available in the interface, is the first step toward creating effective presentations. In this lesson, you will get started with PowerPoint 2010.

You may have scribbled down a fabulous idea on a notepad, but you may need to communicate and present that idea dynamically to generate interest from the audience, or get an approval from your management for implementation. The ability to add graphical objects and illustrations provides you with the flexibility to customize presentations to suit your needs. Microsoft PowerPoint 2010 provides various new features that enable you to efficiently create powerful multimedia presentations.

TOPIC A

Identify the Elements of the User Interface

You have heard about the efficiency of the PowerPoint application in presenting information and want to use it. Before using the application, you need to familiarize yourself with its interface. In this topic, you will identify the elements of the PowerPoint interface.

PowerPoint 2010 is an effective tool that allows you to deliver interactive presentations by adding text and graphic elements. Exploring the enhanced layout and interface elements of PowerPoint 2010 will help you create attractive presentations that you can use during important meetings with members of your staff.

Microsoft PowerPoint 2010

Microsoft *PowerPoint* 2010 is an application from the Microsoft Office suite that you can use to create colorful and dynamic presentations to have a visual impact on the audience. Its user-friendly interface not only helps you streamline your work, but also maximizes productivity. Its multimedia capabilities enable you to add pictures, photos, diagrams, images, videos, sounds, transitions, and animations to presentations. It also provides you with enhanced collaborative capabilities that allow you to make editorial suggestions. In addition, you can add comments to presentations without changing the slide or notes content and view the changes made by different users in a single view. The integrated Help feature lets you easily access information on various tasks and features of PowerPoint.

Presentations

Definition:

A *presentation* is a form of communication in which a message or an idea is effectively conveyed to another individual or multiple people simultaneously. A presentation may involve spoken or written words, pictures, illustrations, videos, and sounds to engage the attention of the audience. Presentations are effective tools for discussions, brainstorming sessions, or training in a business or classroom environment.

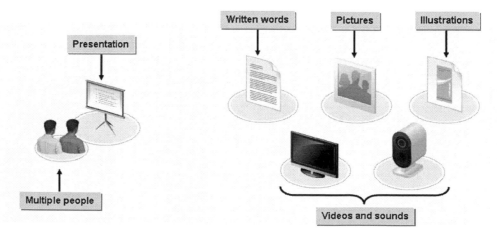

Figure 1-1: *Communicating a message through a presentation.*

Example:

Slides

Slides are presentation objects that are used to display an idea to the target audience. In PowerPoint, a slide uses a defined layout to display the desired content for a presentation. You can display text, graphics, charts, sound files, or even controls on a slide.

Figure 1-2: A slide in Microsoft PowerPoint 2010.

The PowerPoint 2010 Window

The PowerPoint 2010 window displays a variety of interface components that allow you to work effectively and efficiently on your presentations.

Component	Provides
The Quick Access toolbar	Easy access to frequently used commands in the application. It is usually placed above the Ribbon.
The Ribbon	Easy access to various commands available in the application. It is located below the title bar.
The status bar	Basic information about the presentation and quick access to various viewing options.

The Ribbon

The *Ribbon* is a Microsoft Office 2010 user interface component that comprises several task-specific commands grouped together under various tabs. It is designed to be the central location for accessing commands to perform both simple and advanced operations without having to navigate extensively. You can hide the Ribbon by double-clicking an active tab or by clicking the **Minimize the Ribbon** button. The Ribbon can be kept expanded by clicking the pin icon at its top-right corner. Each tab on the Ribbon contains commands that help you perform various PowerPoint functions.

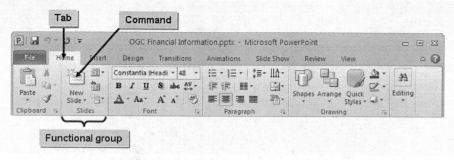

Figure 1-3: *The options available on the Home tab of the Ribbon.*

The Ribbon tabs allow you to access commands that perform simple or advanced operations.

Ribbon Tab	Used to Access
File	Various commands such as **Save, Open, Close, New, Print,** and **Save & Send.** It also displays an interface called the Backstage view that provides commands to perform additional tasks such as changing account settings and managing files.
Home	The most commonly used commands that enable you to perform basic tasks in a presentation. This tab contains functional groups that enable you to create and format a presentation.
Insert	Options to work with different object types such as charts, tables, or pictures that can be added to a presentation.
Design	Several options that help you enhance the visual appeal of a presentation.
Transitions	Options to specify slide transitions.
Animations	Options to add animation effects to slides, or to individual components such as tables or charts.
Slide Show	Options that enable you to deliver a presentation and create custom presentations.
Review	Various options that enable you to review and edit the content in a presentation.
View	Various options that enable you to switch between different presentation views.

ScreenTips

A *ScreenTip* is a text description that is displayed when you hover the mouse pointer over a command or button. It displays the name of a command or style option and may include a description of a command.

KeyTips

If you prefer to use a keyboard to access commands in the PowerPoint interface, press **Alt** to display the corresponding KeyTip for the commands in the current view. To hide KeyTips, press **Alt** again.

Dialog Box Launchers

Dialog box launchers are small buttons with downward pointing arrows located at the bottom-right corner of certain command groups on the Ribbon tabs. They allow you to launch dialog boxes with commands that are specific to the features found in that group. These dialog boxes provide advanced options to adjust the settings that are not available on the Ribbon. Dialog box launchers are grayed-out until an appropriate slide element is selected.

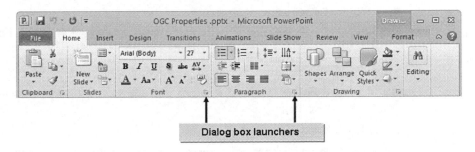

Figure 1-4: *Dialog box launchers used to launch dialog boxes containing specific commands.*

The Backstage View

The *Backstage view* is the interface component that is displayed when you select the **File** tab. It contains a series of tabs that group similar commands, and displays various PowerPoint options to manage a presentation.

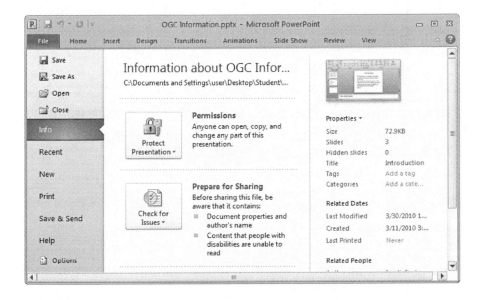

Figure 1-5: *The Backstage view in the PowerPoint 2010 interface.*

Option	Allows You To
Save	Save a newly created presentation, or to save the changes made to an existing presentation.
Save As	Save an existing presentation with a new file name, in a new file format, and in a new location.
Open	Navigate to the location where a presentation is saved and open the file.
Close	Close a file that is open in the PowerPoint application.
Info	Display additional information for a file that is in use.
Recent	Display a list of recently viewed presentations.
New	Create a presentation.
Print	Preview and print a presentation.
Save & Send	Share a presentation to collaborate with others when developing a presentation by using email, SharePoint, or publishing specific slides.
Help	View tutorials and guides that provide information on using PowerPoint.
Options	Display the **PowerPoint Options** dialog box that allows you to customize the way you work with PowerPoint.
Exit	Close the PowerPoint application.

The Quick Access Toolbar

The *Quick Access toolbar* provides easy access to frequently used commands such as **Save, Undo,** and **Redo.** By default, the Quick Access toolbar is placed above the Ribbon to the left of the title bar.

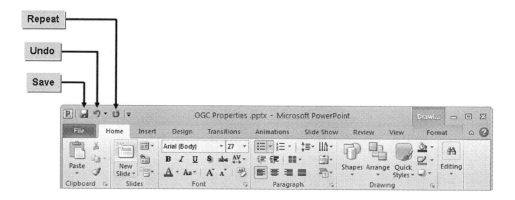

Figure 1-6: Commands on the Quick Access toolbar.

The Status Bar

The *status bar* appears at the bottom of the application window, and displays information about the current slide along with the viewing options for the presentation.

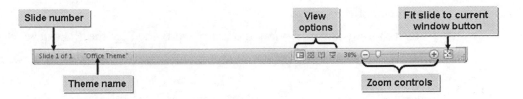

Figure 1-7: Options on the status bar.

Status Bar Option	Description
Slide number	Displays the slide number of the selected slide and the total number of slides in a presentation.
Theme name	Displays the name of the theme applied to the selected slide.
Spell check	Indicates that there are spelling errors on a slide. Clicking the Spell Check icon displays the **Spelling** dialog box, which offers various options, that help you proof the presentation for spelling and grammar.
View options	Allows you to select the desired view to display the slides in a presentation. The available view options are **Normal, Slide Sorter, Reading,** and **Slide Show.**
Zoom controls	Displays the zoom percentage and allows you to set the zoom level using the zoom slider or the **Fit slide to current window** button.

Contextual Tabs

Contextual tabs are sets of additional tabs containing specialized commands that are displayed when specific object types, such as tables, charts, text, or pictures are selected. The commands on these tabs are displayed on the Ribbon, and they can be used to manipulate, edit, and format a selected object. When you deselect the object, these contextual tabs disappear.

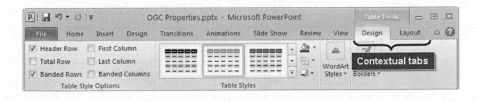

Figure 1-8: Additional tabs displayed when specific object types are selected.

How to Identify the elements of the User Interface

Procedure Reference: Explore the Microsoft PowerPoint 2010 Interface

To explore the Microsoft PowerPoint 2010 interface:

1. Launch the Microsoft PowerPoint 2010 application.
2. Explore the components of the interface.

    -   Select the **File** tab to display and view the options provided by the Backstage view.
    -   On the Quick Access toolbar, hover the mouse pointer over the buttons to view their descriptions.
    -   On the Ribbon, select the tabs to view their groups and commands.
    -   On the status bar, select the desired presentation view to view the presentation.

ACTIVITY 1-1
Exploring the User Interface

Before You Begin:

The desktop is displayed.

Scenario:

You are a new recruit in the finance department of OGC Properties. In your job role, you need to use PowerPoint to create presentations for your department. Because you will be frequently working with PowerPoint, you decide to spend some time in familiarizing yourself with the elements of the user interface.

1. Explore the **File** tab.

   a. Choose **Start→All Programs→Microsoft Office→Microsoft PowerPoint 2010.**

   b. Select the **File** tab to display the Backstage view.

   c. Observe that the commands **Save, Save As, Open, Close, Info, Recent, New, Print, Save & Send, Help, Options,** and **Exit** are displayed in the Backstage view.

   d. On the Ribbon, click the **File** tab to deselect the tab and hide the Backstage view.

2. Explore the Quick Access toolbar.

   a. On the Quick Access toolbar, hover the mouser pointer over the **Save** button, which is placed first from the left, to view its tooltip.

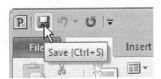

   b. Similarly, view the tooltips for each of the Quick Access toolbar buttons.

   c. Click the **Customize Quick Access Toolbar** drop-down arrow to display the **Customize Quick Access Toolbar** menu.

d. Observe that the **Save, Undo,** and **Redo** check boxes are checked.

e. Click anywhere outside the menu to close the **Customize Quick Access Toolbar** menu.

3. Explore the Ribbon.

a. On the Ribbon, select the **Insert** tab.

b. On the **Insert** tab, in the **Illustrations** group, place the mouse pointer over the **Shapes** button to view its ScreenTip.

c. Select the **Home** tab.

d. On the slide, click in the **Click to add title** text box.

e. On the **Home** tab, in the **Font** group, at the bottom-right corner, click the **Font** dialog box launcher.

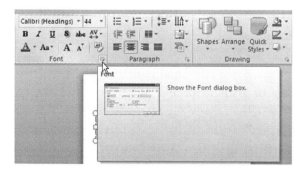

f. Observe that the **Font** dialog box with advanced options to format text is displayed.

g. In the **Font** dialog box, at the top-right corner, click the **Close** button.

h. On the Ribbon, click the **Minimize the Ribbon** button.

i. Click the **Design** tab to expand the Ribbon.

j. At the top-right corner of the Ribbon, click the pin icon to keep the Ribbon expanded.

4. Explore the status bar.

a. On the status bar, on the left side, observe that "Slide 1 of 1" and "Office Theme," which is the default theme are displayed.

b. On the right side, to the left of the **Zoom** slider, hover the mouse pointer over the various buttons and observe the respective ScreenTips.

c. To the left of the **Zoom** slider, click the **Zoom level** button.

d. In the **Zoom** dialog box, in the **Zoom to** section, select **100%** and click **OK** to display the slide in its actual size.

e. On the status bar, on the right side, to the right of the **Zoom** slider, click the **Fit slide to current window** button, to display the complete slide within the application window.

f. Select the **File** tab and choose **Close** to close the presentation.

 In the **Microsoft PowerPoint** message box, click **Don't save** if you do not want to save the changes made to the presentation.

TOPIC B
View Presentations

You explored the PowerPoint 2010 interface. When working with PowerPoint, the ability to view the slides of a presentation in multiple ways will help you organize and edit the presentation based on your needs. In this topic, you will view a presentation in different ways.

Imagine that you are asked to reorganize slides, as well as edit notes in a presentation. PowerPoint 2010 provides options to display the slides in different views and work in a view that best suits your requirements.

Presentation Views

PowerPoint provides you with four different views that you can use to view and work with presentations.

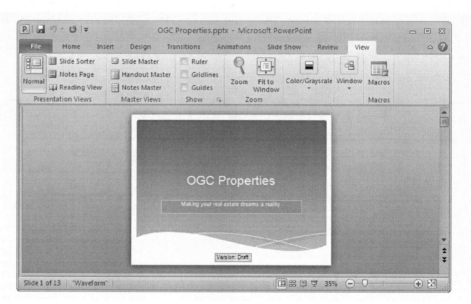

Figure 1-9: *The Normal view.*

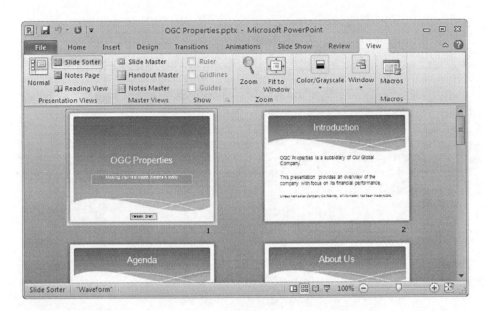

Figure 1-10: The Slide Sorter view.

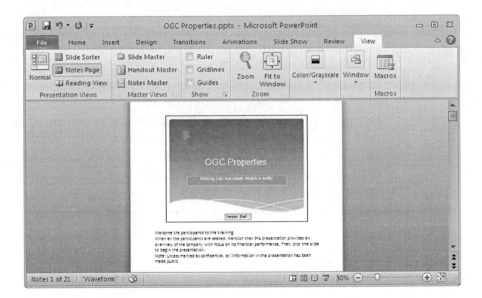

Figure 1-11: The Notes Page view.

Figure 1-12: *The Reading view.*

Presentation View	Description
Normal	Displays all the slides in a presentation. It is the default view in which the PowerPoint application opens.
Slide Sorter	Displays all the slides in a presentation as *thumbnails*. This view makes it easier to arrange slides.
Notes Page	Displays a slide with the slide content and the entire contents of the Notes page. It also enables you to edit the notes content while viewing the entire slide.
Reading	Displays a presentation on screen, one slide at a time within the window, similar to how it will be presented to an audience.

Master Views

The three additional views in the **Master View** group on the **View** tab, Slide Master, Handout Master, and Notes Master, enable you to edit the design and layout of slides, handouts, and notes.

Navigation Methods in the Normal View

PowerPoint allows you to navigate in the Normal view by using a mouse or keyboard shortcut.

Navigation Option	Action
Display a slide	In the left pane, click on the desired slide.
Move to the next slide	In the left pane, select the slide that is placed after the displayed slide, or on the keyboard, press the **Down Arrow** key or **Page Down.**

Navigation Option	Action
Move to the previous slide	In the left pane, select the slide that is placed before the displayed slide, or on the keyboard, press the **Up Arrow** key or **Page Up.**
Move to the beginning of a presentation	In the left pane, scroll up and select the first slide.
Move to the end of a presentation	In the left pane, scroll down and select the last slide.

The Slide Show View

Slide show in PowerPoint displays a presentation on a screen in a sequence. A slide show can be used to brief the audience on important issues that they must make decisions about. Vast amounts of information can be condensed into visual representations and complex issues can be reduced to bullet points to clearly convey vital information. A slide show displays one slide at a time, allowing the audience to follow the narration and quickly grasp critical information.

Navigation Methods in the Slide Show View

PowerPoint allows you to navigate in the Slide Show view by using a mouse or keyboard shortcut.

Navigation Option	Mouse Action	Keyboard Shortcut
Start a presentation from the beginning	Select the **Slide Show** tab, and in the **Start Slide Show** group, click **From Beginning.**	Press **F5.**
Start a presentation from the current slide	Select the **Slide Show** tab, and in the **Start Slide Show** group, click **From Current Slide.**	Press **Shift+F5.**
Go to a specific slide	Right-click the slide, choose **Go to Slide,** and choose **Slide Name.**	Press **<Slide number> + ENTER.**
Advance to the next slide	Click the slide.	Press **N, ENTER, PAGE DOWN, RIGHT ARROW, DOWN ARROW,** or **SPACEBAR.**
Return to the previous slide	Right-click the slide and choose **Previous.**	Press **P, PAGE UP, LEFT ARROW, UP ARROW,** or **Backspace.**
End a presentation	Right-click a slide and choose **End Show.**	Press **ESC.**

The Slides Tab

The *Slides tab,* in the left pane of a presentation displays slides as thumbnails. You can navigate to a specific slide by clicking it or navigate through the entire presentation by using the **Slides** tab scroll bar. You can also arrange slides by dragging individual slides to different locations.

The Outline Tab

The *Outline tab* displays only the text on each slide in a presentation. All text on a slide, including the title, subtitle, and bullets are displayed in a list. You can edit the text on the slides directly on this tab.

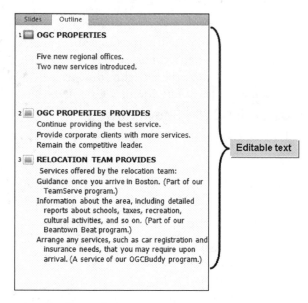

Figure 1-13: Text displayed on the Outline tab.

The Protected View

In Office 2010, files that come from a potentially unsafe source, such as the Internet or an email attachment, are displayed in the Protected view by default. The editing options are disabled in a file that is displayed in the Protected view. Clicking the **Enable Editing** button on the Trust bar at the top of the application window allows you to edit the file. Once you enable editing, the file will no longer be displayed in the Protected view.

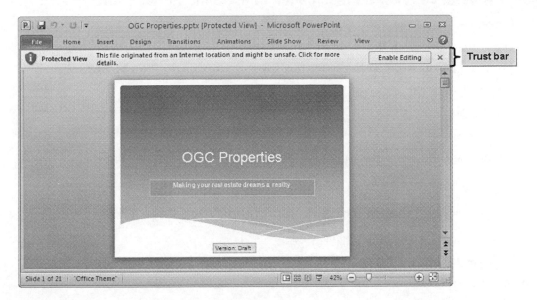

Figure 1-14: *A file displayed in the Protected view.*

How to View Presentations

Procedure Reference: View a Presentation in the Normal View

To view a presentation in the Normal view:

1. Display a presentation in the Normal view.

   - On the **View** tab, in the **Presentation Views** group, click **Normal** or;
   - On the status bar, click the **Normal** button.

2. Navigate through the slides.

   - Use the scroll bar on either the **Slides** tab or the **Outline** tab or;
   - Use the **Slide** pane scroll bar or;
   - Use keyboard shortcuts.

 To get help on keyboard shortcuts to navigate in a presentation, refer to the PowerPoint Help article, "Keyboard shortcuts for use while creating a presentation in PowerPoint 2010."

3. If necessary, at the upper-right corner of the **Slides/Outline** tab, click the close box to hide the pane.

 To display the **Slides/Outline** tab again, display the presentation in the Normal view again.

Procedure Reference: View a Presentation in the Slide Sorter View

To view a presentation in the Slide Sorter view:

1. Display a presentation in the Slide Sorter view.
    *   On the **View** tab, in the **Presentation Views** group, click **Slide Sorter** or;
    *   On the status bar, click the **Slide Sorter** button.
2. Navigate through the slides.
    *   Use the scroll bar or;
    *   Right-click the scroll bar to access the scroll bar shortcut menu or;
    *   Use keyboard shortcuts.

Procedure Reference: View a Presentation in the Notes Page View

To view a presentation in the Notes Page view:

1. On the **View** tab, in the **Presentation Views** group, click **Notes Page.**
2. Navigate through the slides and view the notes.
    *   Use the scroll bar or;
    *   Right-click the scroll bar to access the scroll bar shortcut menu and select the desired option or;
    *   Use keyboard shortcuts.

Procedure Reference: View a Presentation in the Reading View

To view a presentation in the Reading view:

1. On the **View** tab, in the **Presentation Views** group, click **Reading View.**
2. Navigate through the slides.
    *   Use the scroll bar or;
    *   Right-click in the presentation to access the **Slide Show** shortcut menu or;
    *   Use the left mouse button.

Procedure Reference: Run a Slide Show

To run a slide show:

1. Start a slide show.
    *   On the Ribbon, select the **Slide Show** tab, and in the **Start Slide Show** group, select the desired option or;
    *   On the status bar, click the **Slide Show** button.
2. View the slide show by clicking each slide to proceed to the next slide.
3. End the slide show.
    *   Right-click on a slide and choose **End Show** or;
    *   Press **Esc.**

ACTIVITY 1-2
Navigating Through a Presentation

Data Files:

C:\084592Data\Getting Started with PowerPoint\Relocation Team.pptx

Before You Begin:

The PowerPoint application is open.

Scenario:

Your manager has just delivered a presentation, and you took down some notes that will help you while working on presentations in the future. Because you only had a few minutes to look at the presentation, you decide to take a second look to view specific slides again.

---

1. Open a presentation in the Normal view and navigate through it.

   a. Select the **File** tab, and choose **Open.**

   b. In the **Open** dialog box, navigate to the C:\084592Data\Getting Started with PowerPoint folder.

   c. Select the **Relocation Team.pptx** file and click **Open.**

   d. Observe that the first slide is displayed and the thumbnail of the slide in the left pane matches with the slide that is displayed.

   e. In the left pane, on the **Slides** tab, click slide 3 to view its contents.

   f. In the left pane, select the **Outline** tab.

   g. Observe that the title and bullets are displayed in a list format.

---

2. View slides in the Slide Sorter view.

a. Select the **View** tab, and in the **Presentation Views** group, click **Slide Sorter** to view slides as thumbnails.

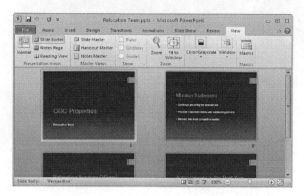

b. In the Slide Sorter view, double-click slide 1 to display it in the Normal view.

3. View the notes page for the Mission Statement slide.

a. In the left pane, select the **Slides** tab and click slide 2.

b. On the **View** tab, in the **Presentation Views** group, click **Notes Page.**

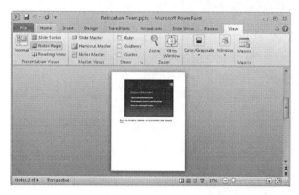

c. View the notes for the slide in the Notes text area.

4. Run the slide show.

a. On the status bar, click the **Slide Show** button.

b. Observe that the slide show starts from slide 2 because you clicked the **Slide Show** button on this slide.

c. Click the slide to view the next slide.

d. Right-click the slide and choose **Go to Slide→1 OGC Properties** to display slide 1.

e. Right-click on the slide and choose **End Show.**

f. On the **View** tab, in the **Presentation Views** group, click **Normal.**

TOPIC C
Save a Presentation

You explored the different presentation views in PowerPoint. To easily access a presentation with different versions of PowerPoint, you may need to save the presentation in an appropriate file format. In this topic, you will save a presentation.

Sometimes, you might find that the most basic task may be the most critical. Working for hours to create a presentation and then forgetting to save it can be very costly. Once you save a presentation, all the work is preserved. Also, if you use older versions of PowerPoint to view these files, you may need to know which features of PowerPoint are compatible with the earlier version so that you can avoid any compatibility issues.

The Save Command

The **Save** command allows you to save a newly created presentation, or to save the changes that you make to an existing presentation. When saving a file for the first time, you are prompted to enter a file name for the presentation and mention the location in which you want to save the file. When you save changes to an existing file, you are not prompted for any information; the changes automatically get saved to the same file and you can close the file or continue working with it. By default, a PowerPoint 2010 presentation is saved in the PPTX file format.

The Save As Option

The **Save As** option allows you to save an existing presentation with a new file name, in a different file format, or in a new location. You can select the desired file format to save the file from the **Save as Type** drop-down list.

File Format	Description
PowerPoint **Presentation**.pptx	A presentation that can be opened only in PowerPoint 2010 or PowerPoint 2007.
PDF.pdf	An electronic file format developed by Adobe Systems that preserves document formatting and enables file sharing.
XPS Document.xps	An electronic paper format for exchanging documents in their final form.
Outline/RTF.rtf	A presentation outline as a text-only document that provides smaller file sizes and the ability to share macro-free files with others who may not have the PowerPoint software. The notes text is not saved with the file.
Open Document Presentation.odp	An OpenDocument Presentation format used by applications, such as Google Docs and OpenOffice.org Impress. You can open presentations in the .odp format in PowerPoint 2010.
PowerPoint Picture Presentation.pptx	A PowerPoint 2010 or 2007 presentation where each slide is converted into a picture. Saving a file as a PowerPoint Picture presentation may reduce the file size. However, some information may1 be lost.
PowerPoint Show.ppsx	A presentation that always opens in the Slide Show view rather than in the Normal view.

The Save vs. Save As Command

The **Save** command overwrites an existing file, whereas the **Save As** command creates a copy of the file with the required changes and leaves the original file intact.

PowerPoint 2010 File Types

Microsoft Office 2010 uses eXtensible Markup Language (XML) as the default file format for storing information in files. A PowerPoint 2010 file can be identified with the letter "x" at the end of the file extension. The default file extension for a PowerPoint 2010 presentation is .pptx. PowerPoint 2010 allows you to save files as presentations, templates, and slide shows.

File Type	*Description*
Presentation	PPTX is the default file type for a PowerPoint 2010 presentation.
	● PPTM is the file type for macro-enabled PowerPoint 2010 presentations.
	● PPT is the file type that is compatible with the previous versions of PowerPoint.
Template	POTX is the default file type for a PowerPoint 2010 template.
	● POTM is the file type for a macro-enabled PowerPoint 2010 template.
	● POT is the file type that is compatible with the previous versions of PowerPoint.
	● THMX is the file type for PowerPoint 2010 theme templates.
Slide show	PPSX is the file type for a PowerPoint 2010 slide show.
	● PPSM is the file type for a macro-enabled PowerPoint 2010 slide show.
	● PPS is the slide show file type that is compatible with previous versions of PowerPoint.

Benefits of XML

The PowerPoint XML format offers significant benefits including:

● Smaller file size—the new format uses zip compression to reduce file size.

● Improved information recovery—files are structured modularly so that they can be opened even if a component within a file is damaged.

● Easier detection of macros—distinct file names make a macro-enabled file easy to recognize.

● Information integration and interoperability—information created within Office applications can easily be shared with other applications.

The Compatibility Checker Feature

The *Compatibility Checker* feature enables you to identify objects such as charts, shapes, and SmartArt graphics used in a PowerPoint 2010 presentation that may not be compatible with previous versions of PowerPoint. Any object that is not compatible will be converted into a picture so that it is displayed correctly in the earlier versions of PowerPoint. Once these objects are converted, they cannot be edited.

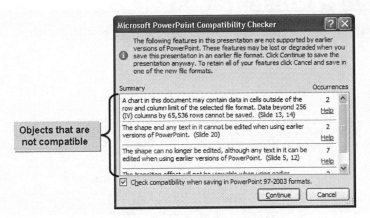

Figure 1-15: Objects that are not compatible with previous versions of PowerPoint.

Presentation Recovery Options

In the course of working on a presentation, if your computer crashes, or an unexpected error interrupts your work, you run the risk of losing unsaved data. On restart, PowerPoint recovers the unsaved draft versions of your presentation in the **Available file** pane, and you can specify the desired version that you want to retain. You can set the presentation recovery options in the **Save presentations** section on the **Save** tab of the **PowerPoint Options** dialog box.

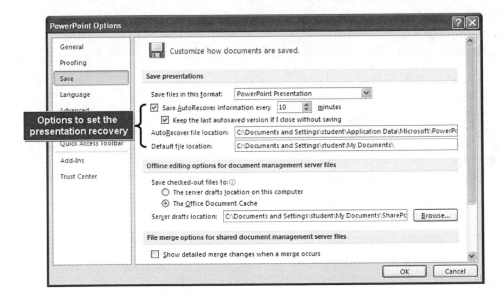

Figure 1-16: Presentation recovery options in the PowerPoint Options dialog box.

How to Save a Presentation

Procedure Reference: Save Changes to an Existing Presentation

To save changes to an existing presentation:

1. Open and modify a presentation.
2. Save the changes.
   - Select the **File** tab and choose **Save** or;
   - On the Quick Access toolbar, click the **Save** button or;
   - Press **Ctrl+S**.

 When you save a new presentation, the **Save As** dialog box is displayed allowing you to specify the file name and location of the new presentation.

Procedure Reference: Save a Presentation Using the Save As Dialog Box

To save a presentation using the **Save As** dialog box:

1. Select the **File** tab and choose **Save As.**
2. In the **Save As** dialog box, navigate to the desired folder.
3. In the **File name** text box, type the name of the file.
4. If necessary, from the **Save as type** drop-down list, select the desired file type.
5. Click **Save.**

Procedure Reference: Save Slides in a Presentation as Pictures

To save slides in a presentation as pictures:

1. Select the **File** tab and choose **Save As.**
2. If necessary, from the **Save as type** drop-down list, select the desired picture format and click **Save.**
3. In the **Microsoft PowerPoint** message box, select the desired option.
   - Select **Every Slide** to save all the slides in the presentation as pictures.
   - Select **Current Slide Only** to save the current slide as a picture.

Procedure Reference: Check a Presentation for Compatibility

To check a presentation for compatibility:

1. Select the **File** tab, and in the Backstage view, choose **Info.**
2. In the **Prepare for Sharing** section, from the **Check for Issues** drop-down list, select **Check Compatibility** to display the **Microsoft PowerPoint Compatibility Checker** dialog box.
3. In the **Microsoft PowerPoint Compatibility Checker** dialog box, click the **Help** button to view details on any compatibility issue you want to resolve.
4. Close the PowerPoint Help window.
5. In the **Microsoft PowerPoint Compatibility Checker** dialog box, click **Continue** to continue with the check.
6. Click **OK** to close the dialog box.

Compatibility Checker Automation

By default, the **Compatibility Checker** opens automatically when you save a file in an earlier version of PowerPoint.

ACTIVITY 1-3
Saving Presentations

Before You Begin:

The Relocation Team.pptx file is open.

Scenario:

You want to create a copy of an existing company presentation to take it home, where you can spend more time reviewing it. You need to save the presentation in the PowerPoint 2003 format because you do not have PowerPoint 2010 installed on your home computer. You need to ensure that you will be able to open the file and all the objects will be displayed correctly when you work on the presentation at home.

---

1. Make a copy of the presentation.

    a. Select the **File** tab and choose **Save As.**

    b. In the **Save As** dialog box, in the **File name** text box, type *My Relocation Team*

    c. Click **Save.**

    d. Observe that the new file name "My Relocation Team" is displayed on the title bar.

    My Relocation Team.pptx - Microsoft PowerPoint

---

2. Save the presentation in the PPT format.

    a. Select the **File** tab and choose **Save As.**

    b. In the **Save As** dialog box, in the **File name** text box, type *My Relocation Team 2003*

    c. From the **Save as type** drop-down list, select **PowerPoint 97–2003 Presentation (*.ppt).**

    d. Click **Save.**

---

3. Check for compatibility.

    a. In the **Microsoft PowerPoint Compatibility Checker** dialog box, verify that the **Check compatibility when saving in PowerPoint 97–2003 formats** check box is checked, and in the **Microsoft PowerPoint Compatibility Checker** dialog box, click **Continue** to save the file with the compatibility issue.

    b. Observe that the title of the presentation at the top of the window is now displayed as "My Relocation Team 2003 [Compatibility Mode] Microsoft PowerPoint."

    c. Select the **File** tab and choose **Close.**

TOPIC D
Use Microsoft PowerPoint Help

You saved a presentation. When you start using PowerPoint, you may come across tools and options that are unfamiliar to you, resulting in delays. In this topic, you will use PowerPoint Help to get assistance when you have a query.

PowerPoint's built-in Help system enables you to find answers to PowerPoint-related questions. As a result, you no longer need to rely on your coworkers or on technical support. You can also use the Help feature to increase your knowledge of PowerPoint.

PowerPoint Help

PowerPoint Help is a repository of information about the functionality of various features of Microsoft PowerPoint 2010. You can search for information on any topic in PowerPoint by specifying your query in the **Search** text box. You can specify whether to search for help information online or from your computer.

Option	Description
The **PowerPoint Help** toolbar	Allows you to access navigational commands.
The **Type words to search for** text box	Allows you to type keywords for which you need to search for information. Previously typed keywords can be found in the Search criteria drop-down list.
The **Search** drop-down list	Allows you to search PowerPoint Help for information from online or offline content with the help of the options provided, based on the criterion that you have chosen.
The **Browse PowerPoint Help** pane	Displays the topics available in PowerPoint Help in a tabular form. You can navigate to a topic by clicking it.

Areas of Search

You can specify a search area to narrow down the search results. You can either use the Help repository on your computer or select the **Content from Office Online** option to search the web for help.

Area of Search	Lists
All PowerPoint	Information on the query from the built-in Help feature and provides help links from the Microsoft Office website, if required.
PowerPoint Help	Information on the query from the built-in Help feature as well as the Microsoft Office website, but does not take you to the Office website.
PowerPoint Templates	Templates that are available from the Microsoft Office website.
PowerPoint Training	Training information links from the Microsoft Office website.

Area of Search	Lists
Developer Reference	Programming tasks, samples, and references to guide you in developing customized solutions, based on PowerPoint.

PowerPoint Help Toolbar Options

The **PowerPoint Help** toolbar provides buttons that enable you to quickly navigate through the Help system.

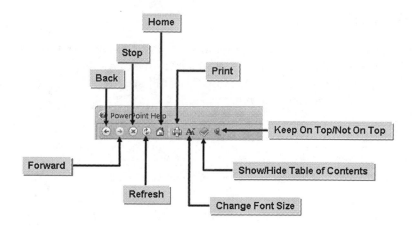

Figure 1-17: Options to navigate through the Help system.

Button	Used To
Back	Navigate to the page that was previously accessed.
Forward	Navigate to the next page. The **Forward** button is enabled only after the **Back** button has been used.
Stop	Stop the search that is in progress.
Refresh	Refresh the page that is displayed.
Home	Display the **Home** page of PowerPoint Help.
Print	Print a **Help** page with specific options.
Change Font Size	Increase or decrease the font size of the text in a Help topic.
Show/Hide Table of Contents	Display the task pane, which contains the table of contents of PowerPoint Help.
Keep On Top/Not On Top	Set the Help window to stay on top of other PowerPoint windows or display other PowerPoint windows on top of the Help window.

How to Use Microsoft PowerPoint Help

Procedure Reference: Search Using Microsoft PowerPoint Help

To search using Microsoft PowerPoint Help:

1. Access Microsoft PowerPoint Help.

   - In the application window, at the upper-right corner, click the **PowerPoint Help** button or;

   - Press **F1.**

2. In the **Type words to search for** text box, type a word or phrase.

3. If necessary, from the **Search** drop-down list, select an option to specify the search area.

4. Click **Search** to display the search results.

5. In the **Browse PowerPoint Help** pane, click a link to view the description.

ACTIVITY 1-4

Using the Microsoft PowerPoint Help Feature

Before You Begin:

The PowerPoint application is open.

Scenario:

As a new user of PowerPoint, you are not sure about a few of the features that you came across while exploring the application. You want to access the resources that will provide necessary information to familiarize yourself with the application.

1. Find information on the new features in PowerPoint 2010.

   a. Select the **File** tab and choose **New.**

   b. Verify that in the **Available Templates and Themes** pane, in the **Home** section, **Blank presentation** is selected, and in the **Blank presentation** section, click **Create** to create a new presentation.

   c. On the Ribbon, at the top-right corner, click the **Microsoft PowerPoint Help** button.

   d. Maximize the PowerPoint Help window.

   e. In the PowerPoint Help window, in the **Browse PowerPoint Help** section, click the **What's new** link.

   f. In the **Topics** section, click the **What's new in PowerPoint 2010** link.

   g. Observe the details of the new features displayed in the PowerPoint Help window.

2. Search for information about the Ribbon.

   a. In the PowerPoint Help window, in the **Type words to search for** text box, click and type *ribbon* and then click **Search.**

   b. In the displayed results, click the **Familiarize yourself with the ribbon in PowerPoint 2010** link to access the page that describes the Ribbon.

   c. Observe that the information about the Ribbon is displayed.

   d. On the toolbar, click the **Back** button to display the previous page.

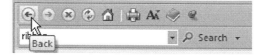

   e. Close the PowerPoint Help window.

Lesson 1 Follow-up

In this lesson, you familiarized yourself with various options available in the PowerPoint 2010 interface and created basic presentations. Getting acquainted with the user interface and creating basic presentations will give you the confidence to use advanced options to create more complex presentations.

1. **When you create a presentation, what is most important to you: the overall look, the information it contains, or the mode of its delivery?**

2. **Do you think it's important to be able to save presentations in different file formats?**

2 Creating a Basic Presentation

Lesson Time: 1 hour(s), 30 minutes

Lesson Objectives:

In this lesson, you will create a basic presentation.

You will:

- Select a presentation type.
- Enter text.
- Edit text.
- Format text placeholders.
- Add slides to a presentation.
- Arrange slides.
- Work with themes.

Introduction

You are familiar with the PowerPoint 2010 interface. You may now want to present information in the form of a presentation. In this lesson, you will create a basic PowerPoint presentation.

By sharing information through presentations, you can keep your audience engaged. PowerPoint tools enable you to create presentations that can be customized to suit different situations. By creating a basic presentation, you can create a framework that can be used to build complex presentations.

TOPIC A
Select a Presentation Type

You used the PowerPoint Help feature to access help resources. You now want to get started with creating a presentation by determining how you want to present information. In this topic, you will select a presentation type.

Often, business presentations have to be created at short notice and tight schedules. Knowledge of various ways of creating a presentation will allow you to decide how you want to get started with creating a presentation. PowerPoint provides you with different techniques to minimize the design time and effectively undertake creating presentations from scratch or by using a template as a base to build presentations.

Templates

Definition:

A *template* is a preformatted file that is used as a model from which to base other files, such as documents and slides. A PowerPoint template contains predefined design elements, such as graphics and text. It also has predefined settings for color schemes, styles, backgrounds, and fonts. By using a template, you can create documents that share common design elements.

Example:

Figure 2-1: Templates with graphics and text.

Methods for Creating a Presentation

PowerPoint provides you with six options based on which you can create a presentation.

Option	Creates
Blank presentation	A presentation with a single blank slide containing Title formatting by default.
Recent templates	A presentation based on a recently used template.
Sample templates	A presentation based on a predefined template. It can contain sample text and images to help users get started.
Themes	A presentation from a theme.
My templates	A presentation based on a template that is marked as a favorite.
New from existing	A presentation based on a previously saved presentation.

How to Select a Presentation Type

Procedure Reference: Open a New Presentation

To select a presentation from available templates and themes:

1. Select the **File** tab and choose **New.**
2. In the **Available Templates and Themes** pane, select the desired option.
   - Select **Blank presentation** and click **Create.**
   - Select **Recent templates,** and in the **Recent templates** section, choose a recently used template and then click **Create.**
   - Select **Sample templates,** and in the **Sample templates** section, choose a sample template and click **Create.**
   - Select **Themes,** and in the **Themes** section, choose a theme and click **Create.**
   - Select **My templates,** and in the **New Presentation** dialog box, in the **Personal Templates** section, choose a template and click **OK.**
   - Select **New from existing,** and in the **New From Existing Presentation** dialog box, navigate to the required folder, choose the desired file, and click **Create New.**

ACTIVITY 2-1
Creating a Template-Based Presentation

Before You Begin:
Microsoft PowerPoint 2010 is open.

Scenario:
You work for the real estate division of Our Global Company (OGC). For the upcoming annual staff meeting, you need to create a presentation that is to be used by the CEO during his address. This presentation includes critical business information about OGC Properties, its business priorities, financial status, and key focus areas. Before doing this, you want to choose a template that will suit the presentation.

---

1. Display the available templates in PowerPoint 2010.

   a. Select the **File** tab and choose **New** to display the Backstage view.

   b. In the **Available Templates and Themes** pane, in the **Home** section, click **Sample templates** to display the templates available in PowerPoint 2010.

---

2. Create a presentation based on a template.

   a. In the **Available Templates and Themes** pane, in the **Sample templates** section, select **Introducing PowerPoint 2010.**

   b. In the **Introducing PowerPoint 2010** pane, click **Create.**

   c. Observe that a presentation based on the **Introducing PowerPoint 2010** presentation template is displayed in the Normal view for editing. On the left of the status bar, observe the information that the presentation contains 20 slides.

   d. On the Quick Access toolbar, click **Save.**

   e. Observe that the **Save As** dialog box is displayed when you save a new presentation for the first time, and in the **Save As** dialog box, navigate to the C:\084592Data\ Creating a Basic Presentation folder.

   f. In the **Save As** dialog box, in the **File name** text box, click and type *My Training* and click **Save.**

   g. Select the **File** tab and choose **Close.**

TOPIC B
Enter Text

You initiated a presentation using the various options in PowerPoint. Text plays an important role in most presentations and therefore, you need to know how to add text to slides. In this topic, you will enter text in a slide.

Textual content is an indispensable part of any presentation. If you are not aware of the various ways of entering text in a slide, you will spend considerable time in text alignment and correction when finalizing a presentation. Knowing how to enter text will allow you to enter information by using text from other documents, from slides in the same presentation, or by typing in the text placeholders. Once you are familiar with adding textual content to your slide, you can convey information effectively.

Text Placeholders

A *text placeholder* is a container that holds the text you type. Most slide layouts contain one or more text placeholders that can be moved and positioned on a slide. A text placeholder can contain multiple lines of text that automatically wraps to the next line when the typed text reaches the right margin of the text placeholder. You can resize a text placeholder by dragging the sizing handles. If the amount of text in a text placeholder exceeds its size, the font size and the vertical height of the placeholder are automatically adjusted to accommodate text within the text placeholder. However, PowerPoint also allows you to keep the font size unchanged within a text placeholder.

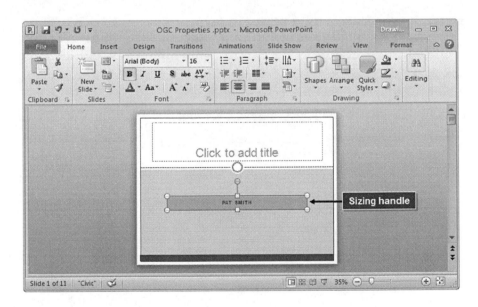

Figure 2-2: Text placeholder on a slide.

Text Boxes

Additional text placeholders can be used on a slide when you need to add text outside the default text placeholders in a slide layout. The **Text Box** button in the **Text** group on the **Insert** tab is used to insert a text box. You can also insert a text box by pasting text on a slide without selecting any text placeholders on the slide. Additional text boxes can be resized and repositioned as desired. If you click outside a text box before entering text, the text box disappears.

How to Enter Text

Procedure Reference: Enter Text in a Text Placeholder

To enter text in a text placeholder:

1. In the left pane, on the **Slides** tab, select the slide to which you want to add text.
2. Click in a text placeholder and type text.

Procedure Reference: Insert a Text Box

To insert a text box:

1. Navigate to the slide where you want to insert a text box.
2. On the **Insert** tab, in the **Text** group, click **Text Box.**
3. On the slide, click at the desired location and drag to create a text box of the desired size.
4. In the text box, type the desired text.
5. If necessary, click the resize handle and drag to resize the text box as desired.
6. If necessary, click the border of the text box and drag it to the desired location.

Procedure Reference: Delete a Text Placeholder

To delete a text placeholder:

1. Navigate to a slide that contains the text placeholder you want to delete.
2. Click the border of the text placeholder to select it.
3. Press **Delete** to delete the placeholder and the text within it.

ACTIVITY 2-2
Entering Text

Before You Begin:
The Microsoft PowerPoint application window is open.

Scenario:
You want to create a new presentation for OGC Properties. To start with, you decide to add introductory details that are relevant to the presentation in the title slide.

---

1. Add information to the title slide.

   a. Select the **File** tab and choose **New.**

   b. In the **Available Templates and Themes** pane, in the **Home** section, verify that **Blank presentation** is selected, and in the **Blank presentation** pane, click **Create.**

   c. On the slide, click in the **Click to add title** text placeholder and type *OGC Properties*

   d. Click in the **Click to add subtitle** text placeholder and type *Making your real estate dreams a reality*

---

2. Add a text box to display the version of the presentation.

   a. Select the **Insert** tab, and in the **Text** group, click **Text Box.**

   b. Below the "Making your real estate dreams a reality" text placeholder, click to create a new text box and type *Version: Draft*

   c. Click outside the text box to deselect it.

---

3. Resize the text placeholder containing the mission text.

   a. On the slide, click before the text "Making your real estate dreams a reality" to display the text placeholder.

b. Select the bottom middle sizing handle and drag it up to just below the text "Making your real estate dreams a reality."

c. On the Quick Access toolbar, click the **Save** button.

d. In the **Save As** dialog box, in the **File name** text box, type **My OGC Properties** and click **Save.**

e. Select the **File** tab and choose **Close** to close the presentation.

TOPIC C
Edit Text

You entered text in a presentation. You may want to ensure that the text on a slide is correct to convey information effectively. In this topic, you will edit text on slides.

Presentations often evolve through the creation process and require a good deal of restructuring before reaching their final forms. Editing text allows you to effectively convey your ideas. By understanding the options for editing text, you will be able to modify the text on a slide to convey your ideas accurately and effectively.

Text Selection Methods

PowerPoint provides you with various text selection methods that allow you to select text on a slide.

To Select	Do This
Variable amounts of text	• Click and drag the mouse pointer to select a block of text. • Place the insertion point at the beginning of the text, hold down **Shift**, and press an arrow key to extend the selection in the desired direction. • Place the insertion point at the beginning of the text, hold down **Shift**, and click at the end of the desired block of text.
A word	Double-click the word. This selects the trailing space after the word, but does not select the punctuation mark after it.
A sentence	Triple-click the sentence.
Noncontiguous sections (items that are not adjacent)	Select the first item, line, or paragraph and hold down **Ctrl** while you select additional items.
The entire slide	• Press **Ctrl+A.** • On the **Home** tab, in the **Editing** group, from the **Select** drop-down list, select **Select All.**

 To deselect text, make another selection, or click away from the selected text anywhere on the slide.

The Mini Toolbar

The *Mini toolbar* is a floating toolbar that appears beside the selected text, and consists of commonly used text formatting options such as font face, size, color, bold, italics, and alignment. You can use any of these options without having to access the commands on the Ribbon. The Mini toolbar disappears when you move the mouse pointer away from the toolbar or the selected text. You can also invoke the Mini toolbar, along with a list of other commands by right-clicking anywhere in a text placeholder.

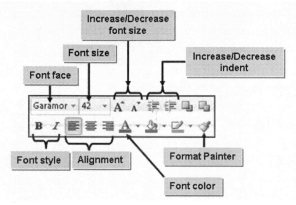

Figure 2-3: *Options on the Mini toolbar.*

The Cut, Copy, and Paste Options

PowerPoint allows you to copy or move text within a slide, across slides, between presentations, and from PowerPoint to other applications or vice versa. You can use the **Cut, Copy,** and **Paste** buttons available in the **Clipboard** group on the **Home** tab to cut, copy, or paste text.

The **Cut** button allows you to remove selected text, while the **Copy** button allows you to copy text. The text you cut or copy will be temporarily stored in the clipboard. You can then place the text in a new location by clicking the **Paste** button. Alternatively, you can move a selected piece of text by dragging it onto a new location, or copy by holding **Ctrl** while dragging the selected text.

Alternate Methods to Cut, Copy, and Paste Text

The **Cut, Copy,** and **Paste** options can also be accessed from the shortcut menu that is displayed when you right-click the selected text. In addition, you can use the **Ctrl+X, Ctrl+C,** and **Ctrl+V** shortcut keys to cut, copy, and paste text, respectively.

The Clipboard

The clipboard in Office 2010 stores all items that you cut or copy. You can view the **Clipboard** task pane by clicking the **Clipboard** dialog box launcher in the **Clipboard** group of the **Home** tab. You can copy items to the clipboard from other Office applications. To paste an item from the clipboard onto a slide, you just have to click the item in the **Clipboard** task pane.

The **Paste All** and **Clear All** buttons in this task pane enable you to paste or remove all the items in the clipboard, respectively.

Paste Options

You can paste text or sections of text that are copied or cut, in any part of a slide, by using the paste options in the **Clipboard** group.

Paste Option	Effect
Use Destination Theme	The pasted text will acquire the formatting of the theme applied to the destination placeholder.
Keep Source Formatting	The pasted text will retain the formatting of the source text placeholder.
Keep Text Only	Only the unformatted text will be pasted.

The Paste Preview Option

Paste Preview is an option that enables a temporary live preview when a **Paste** command is used. The live preview that is displayed on a slide gives you an idea as to how your slide will look when content is pasted. The preview updates the display for each of the paste options available in the **Paste** drop-down list.

Galleries

Galleries are libraries of options that display the varying outcomes of using certain commands on the Ribbon. The options in a gallery are displayed as thumbnails and offer a live preview when you hover the mouse pointer over an option. Most of the functional groups on the Ribbon have galleries, which provide you with a set of predefined styles, that can be applied when working on a presentation.

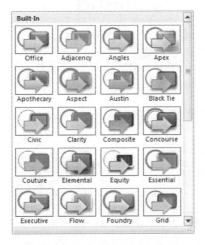

Figure 2-4: *A gallery displaying various predefined styles.*

 Some gallery options are also available on shortcut menus that can be accessed with a right-click.

The Live Preview Feature

The *Live Preview* feature enables you to view the results of the formatting changes without actually applying them. These changes are displayed in real time when you hover the mouse pointer over the available options in a gallery or drop-down list. The temporary formatting disappears when you move the mouse pointer away from the option. This feature helps you avoid the laborious process of applying various commands and setting options in dialog boxes to check for the desired results.

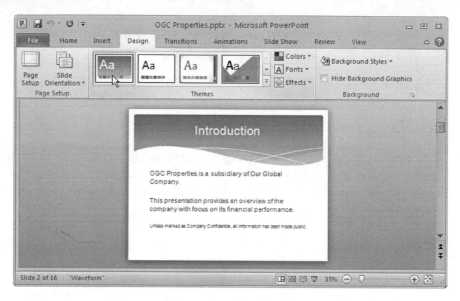

Figure 2-5: A live preview of a selected theme.

The Paste Special Command

The **Paste Special** command is used to paste items in a new location according to your specifications. The default file format of the object to be pasted will appear selected in the **As** list box in the **Paste Special** dialog box. You can either accept the default file format or select from various formats available in the **As** list box.

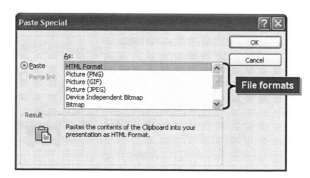

Figure 2-6: The Paste Special dialog box.

How to Edit Text

Procedure Reference: Edit Existing Text

To edit existing text:

1. Locate the text to be edited.
   - Select the text that you want to change.
   - Place the insertion point at the appropriate place.
2. Type the new text.
3. Click outside the text placeholder to deselect it.

Procedure Reference: Delete Text

To delete text:

1. Select the text that you want to delete using the appropriate selection technique.
2. Press **Delete.**

Procedure Reference: Copy, Cut, and Paste Text

To copy, cut, and paste text:

1. Select text from a text placeholder or a text box.
2. Copy text into the clipboard.
   - Copy text into the clipboard by using the appropriate method.
     - On the **Home** tab, click the **Copy** button or;
     - Right-click and choose **Copy** or;
     - Press **Ctrl+C.**
   - Cut text into the clipboard by using the appropriate method.
     - On the **Home** tab, click the **Cut** button or;
     - Right-click and choose **Cut** or;
     - Press **Ctrl+X.**
3. Navigate to the location where you want to paste text.
   - To paste text within a presentation, navigate to the slide where you want to paste it.
   - To paste text into another presentation, open the presentation and navigate to the slide where you want to paste it.
4. On the slide, click in a text placeholder or a text box.
5. Paste text by using the appropriate method.
   - On the **Home** tab, click the **Paste** button or;
   - Right-click and choose **Paste** or;
   - Press **Ctrl+V.**
6. If necessary, click the **Paste Option** button that appears at the right corner of the pasted text and select an option.

Procedure Reference: Paste Text Using the Paste Special Option

To paste text using the **Paste Special** option:

1. Cut or copy the text into the clipboard.
2. Navigate to the location where you want to paste the text.

3. On the slide, click in a text placeholder.

4. On the **Home** tab, in the **Clipboard** group, from the **Paste** drop-down list, select **Paste Special.**

5. In the **Paste Special** dialog box, in the **As** list box, select an option and click **OK.**

Procedure Reference: Duplicate a Text Placeholder

To duplicate a text placeholder:

1. Select the text placeholder.

2. Duplicate the text placeholder.

- On the **Home** tab, in the **Clipboard** group, from the **Paste** drop-down list, select **Duplicate** or;
- Press **Ctrl+D.**

Procedure Reference: Move or Copy Text Using the Drag-and-Drop Method

To move or copy text using the drag-and-drop method:

1. Select text content from the desired file.

2. Move or copy text.

- Click and drag the selected text to the new location on a slide in PowerPoint to move the selected text.
- Hold down **Ctrl** and click and drag the selected text to the new location on a slide in PowerPoint to copy the text.

ACTIVITY 2-3
Editing Slide Text

Data Files:

C:\084592Data\Creating a Basic Information\OGC Financial Information.pptx, C:\084592Data\ Creating a Basic Presentation\OGC Properties - Financial Highlights.docx

1. Open Microsoft Word.

2. Microsoft PowerPoint is open.

Scenario:

You have created a title slide with the name of the organization, mission text, and the version information. You now need to create the presentation based on the content received from your manager. In addition, your colleague has provided you with some interesting information from another presentation. You want to add this information to your presentation.

---

1. Update the text on a slide.

    a.   Navigate to the C:\084592Data\Creating a Basic Presentation folder, select **OGC Properties - Financial Information.pptx,** and click **Open.**

    b.   On slide 2, in the first sentence, double-click the text "part."

    c.   Type *subsidiary* to replace the existing word.

---

2. Move text from one slide to another.

    a.   In the left pane, on slide 2, double-click the text "Agenda" to select it.

    b.   On the **Home** tab, in the **Clipboard** group, click **Cut.**

    c.   On the **Slides** tab, select slide 3.

    d.   On the slide, click the **Click to add title** text placeholder.

    e.   On the **Home** tab, in the **Clipboard** group, click **Paste.**

---

3. Rearrange the text on a slide.

    a.   In the left pane, on the slide, in the fourth sentence, click before the word "Project," hold down **Shift,** and in the fifth sentence, click after the word "Process" in the fourth sentence to select both bullet points.

    b.   Click and drag the selected text after the bullet point "Balance Sheet."

    c.   Click after the letter "t" in the word "Sheet" and press **Enter.**

    d.   Click on the blank line and press **Delete** to remove the empty line.

4.   Copy text from a Word document and paste it on slide 4.

    a.   In the left pane, on the **Slides** tab, select slide 4.

    b.   Switch to the Word document.

    c.   In the Word document, verify that the insertion point is placed before the text "$1.2 million" and press **Ctrl+A.**

    d.   Press **Ctrl+C.**

    e.   Close the OGC Properties - Financial Highlights.docx file.

    f.   Display the Financial Information.pptx file.

    g.   On slide 4, click the text **Click to add text** in the text placeholder.

    h.   Press **Ctrl+V.**

    i.   On the **Paste Options** toolbar, click **Keep Source Formatting.**

    j.   On the **File** tab, choose **Save.**

    k.   In the **Save As** dialog box, in the **File name** text box, type *My OGC Financial Information* and click **Save.**

    l.   Select the **File** tab and choose **Close** to close the presentation.

    m.   Close the Word application.

TOPIC D
Format Text Placeholders

You edited text in a presentation. You may want to modify the properties of text to improve its appearance on the slides. In this topic, you will format text placeholders.

Often, you will have multiple slides in a presentation that look similar with the same text properties. This may make a presentation monotonous. To sustain the interest of the audience, you may want to highlight text on certain slides. PowerPoint allows you to format text placeholders to present text with background colors, outlines, and effects.

Text Placeholder Formatting Options

PowerPoint provides you with various options for formatting a text placeholder or text box.

Option	Allows You To
Shape Fill	Apply a background color to a text placeholder. You can choose from a wide range of colors.
Shape Outline	Apply a color and style to the line that marks the boundaries of a text box. The **Shape Outline** drop-down list contains the **Weight** option to set the line width, and the **Dashes** option to set the line style of the text placeholder.
Shape Effects	Apply multi-dimensional effects to a text box. These effects include **Preset, Shadow, Reflection, Glow, Soft Edges, Bevel,** and **3–D Rotation.**

 When **Shape Fill** is applied, the text in the text box will be displayed with its existing color. Make sure to choose a shape fill color that will retain text visibility.

How to Format Text Placeholders

Procedure Reference: Modify the Appearance of Text Placeholders

To modify the appearance of text placeholders:

1. On a slide, select a text placeholder.

2. On the **Format** contextual tab, in the **Shape Styles** group, select the desired formatting option.

   - In the **Shape Styles** gallery, select the desired theme.

   - Click the **More** button, and from the displayed gallery, select a theme.

   - Click the **Shape Fill** drop-down arrow, and from the displayed gallery, select a background.

     - In the **Theme Colors** or **Standard Colors** section, select a color.

     - In the **Standard Colors** section, click **More Fill Colors,** and in the **Colors** dialog box, on the **Standard** tab, select the desired color and click **OK.**

     - Select **Picture,** and in the **Insert Picture** dialog box, navigate to the picture you want to insert and click **Insert.**

     - Select **Gradient,** and from the displayed gallery, select a gradient from **Light Variations** or **Dark Variations.**

     - Select **Texture,** and from the displayed gallery, select a texture.

   - Click the **Shape Outline** drop-down arrow, and from the displayed gallery, select an outline.

     - In the **Theme Colors** section, choose a color for the outline.

     - In the **Standard Colors** section, choose **Weight,** and from the displayed list, select a line width.

     - In the **Standard Colors** section, choose **Dashes,** and from the displayed list, select a line style.

   - Click the **Shape Effects** drop-down arrow, and from the displayed gallery, select an effect.

     - Select the **Preset,** option, and from the displayed gallery, select an option.

     - Select **Shadow,** and from the displayed gallery, select an option.

     - Select **Reflection,** and from the displayed gallery, select an option to apply the reflection effect to a shape.

     - Select **Glow,** and from the displayed gallery, select an option to apply the glow effect to the edges of a shape.

     - Select **Soft Edges,** and from the displayed gallery, select an option to change the sharpness of the outline of shapes.

     - Select **Bevel,** and from the displayed gallery, select a bevel option.

     - Select **3–D Rotation,** and from the displayed gallery, select an option to change the three-dimensional orientation of a shape.

   - Click the **Format Shape** dialog box launcher, and in the **Format Shape** dialog box, in the left pane, select **Text Box,** and in the right pane, in the **Text Box** section, specify the settings.

3. On the **Home** tab, in the **Paragraph** group, from the **Align Text** drop-down list, select an option to align the text in the placeholder.

4. If necessary, right-click the text placeholder and choose **Set as Default Shape** to set this formatting as default for all new text placeholders.

Procedure Reference: Change the Shape of Text Placeholders

To change the shape of text placeholders:

1. Select the desired text placeholder for which you want to change the shape.

2. On the **Format** tab, in the **Insert Shapes** group, from the **Edit Shape** drop-down list, select **Change Shape.**

3. From the displayed gallery, select the desired shape.

ACTIVITY 2-4
Formatting Text Placeholders

Data Files:

C:\084592Data\Creating a Basic Presentation\My OGC Properties.pptx

Before You Begin:

The PowerPoint application is open˙.

Scenario:

You want the first slide of your presentation to be more visually appealing. So, you decide to format the containers that hold text on the first slide to improve the visual appeal of text within them.

1. Format the version text placeholder.

    a. Navigate to the C:\084592Data\Creating a Basic Presentation folder and open the My OGC Properties.pptx file.

    b. Click before the version text to display the text placeholder.

    c. Click the border of the version text placeholder to select it.

    d. On the **Drawing Tools** tab, select the **Format** contextual tab, and in the **Shape Styles** group, from the **Shape Fill** drop-down list, select **Texture.**

    e. From the displayed gallery, select **Blue tissue paper,** which is the first texture in the fifth row.

    f. In the **Shape Styles** group, click the **Shape Outline** drop-down arrow, and from the displayed gallery, in the **Theme Colors** section, select **Dark Blue, Text 2, Lighter 60%,** which is the fourth style in the third row.

    g. In the **Shape Styles** group, from the **Shape Effects** drop-down list, select **Glow.**

    h. From the displayed gallery, in the **Glow Variations** section, select the **Blue, 8 pt glow, Accent color 1** variation, which is the first variation in the second row.

    i. Click outside the text and observe that the color of the text "Version: Draft" is gray.

2. Format the placeholder that contains the text "Making your real estate dreams a reality."

    a. Triple-click the text "Making your real estate dreams a reality."

    b. Select the **Format** contextual tab, and in the **WordArt Styles** group, click the **Text Fill** drop-down arrow, and from the displayed gallery, in the **Theme Colors** section, select **White, Background,** which is the first color in the first row.

    c. On the **Format** contextual tab, in the **Shape Styles** group, from the **Shape Fill** drop-down list, in the **Theme Colors** section, select **Blue, Accent 1, Lighter 10%,** which is the third color in the third row.

d.   Click the **Shape Outline** drop-down arrow, and from the displayed gallery, in the **Theme Colors** section, select **Dark Blue, Text 2, Lighter 40%,** which is the fourth color in the fourth row.

e.   Save the presentation.

TOPIC E
Add Slides to a Presentation

You formatted text placeholders. You may need to include more content in a presentation to offer the continuity of an idea, which needs to be presented to the audience. In this topic, you will add slides to a presentation.

An effective presentation should have uniform distribution of content across slides. This ensures that too much information is not presented in a single slide, which might be visually jarring and confusing to the audience. After fixing the appearance of slides, distribution of information across slides is necessary. Therefore, you may need to add slides based on the flow of information in a presentation.

Slide Layouts

Definition:

A *slide layout* is a slide template that determines the placement of content on a slide. You can apply a slide layout to existing slides as well as to new slides that are inserted in a presentation. Placeholders that can hold text, tables, charts, and other slide content are built into a layout. When you create a blank presentation, the title slide layout is applied to the first slide of the presentation by default.

Example:

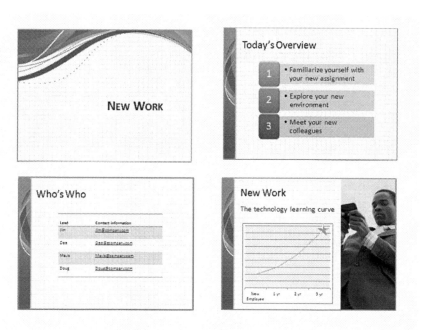

Figure 2-7: A slide template that determines the placement of content on a slide.

Types of Slide Layouts

PowerPoint provides you with different types of slide layouts that can be applied to slides in a presentation.

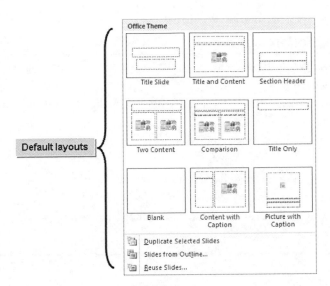

Figure 2-8: *A slide template that determines the placement of content on a slide.*

Slide Layout Type	Provides
Title Slide	Text placeholders to enter a main title and a subtitle.
Title and Content	A placeholder to enter title text and a placeholder to populate content in the slide that can include text, charts, tables, pictures, clip art, and SmartArt graphics.
Section Header	Text placeholders to enter section and subsection titles.
Two Content	A placeholder to enter title text and two content placeholders to populate content that can include text, charts, tables, pictures, clip art, and SmartArt graphics.
Comparison	A placeholder to enter title text, two text placeholders to enter subtitles, and two content placeholders to populate content that can include text, charts, tables, pictures, clip art, and SmartArt graphics.
Title Only	A text placeholder to enter title text.
Blank	A blank slide with no placeholders.
Content with Caption	A placeholder to enter title text, a text placeholder to enter text, and a content placeholder to populate content that can include text, charts, tables, pictures, clip art, and SmartArt graphics.
Picture with Caption	A picture placeholder to insert a picture and a text placeholder to enter caption text.

The Reuse Slides Pane

PowerPoint enables you to share and reuse slides in your presentation by selecting options from the **Reuse Slides** pane.

Option	Description
The **Insert slide from** text box	Allows you to type a path to navigate to a presentation from which you want to reuse slides.
The **Browse** drop-down list	Allows you to browse for slides from a slide library or from existing presentations.
The **Open a Slide Library** link	Allows you to access slides from a slide library.
The **Open a PowerPoint File** link	Allows you to access slides from a PowerPoint file.
The **Learn more about reusing slides** link	Allows you to access help topics pertaining to reusing slides.

How to Add Slides to a Presentation

Procedure Reference: Add a Slide to a Presentation

To add a slide to a presentation:

1. Open the desired presentation.
2. Add a slide to the presentation.
   - In the left pane, on the **Slides** tab, right-click on the desired location and choose **New Slide.**
   - On the **Home** tab, in the **Slides** group, click the **New Slide** drop-down arrow, and from the displayed gallery, in the **Office Theme** section, select a layout to insert the new slide with the selected layout.
   - Duplicate the desired slide.
     - Right-click the desired slide and choose **Duplicate Slide** or;
     - On the **Home** tab, in the **Slides** group, from the **New Slide** drop-down list, select **Duplicate Selected Slides.**

Procedure Reference: Change the Layout of an Existing Slide

To change the layout of an existing slide:

1. Select the slide for which you want to change the layout.
2. On the **Home** tab, in the **Slides** group, click the **Layout** drop-down arrow, and from the displayed gallery, select a new layout.

 When you change a slide layout that has text or graphics, the existing text and graphics are moved on the slide into the new placeholder locations. No content on the slide is deleted, even if there are no placeholders available on the new layout.

Procedure Reference: Reuse Slides from an Existing Presentation

To reuse slides from an existing presentation:

1. On the **Home** tab, in the **Slides** group, from the **New Slide** drop-down list, select **Reuse Slides.**

2. In the **Reuse Slides** pane, specify the location of the existing presentation.

   - In the **Insert slide from** text box, enter the location of the slide library, and to the right of the **Insert slide from** text box, click the arrow button to locate the slide library.

   - From the **Browse** drop-down list, select **Browse Slide Library,** and in the **Select a Slide Library** dialog box, select a slide library and then click **Select.**

   - From the **Browse** drop-down list, select **Browse File,** and in the **Browse** dialog box, navigate to a folder, select a file, and click **Open.**

3. If desired, in the **Reuse Slides** pane, check the **Keep Source Formatting** check box.

4. In the **Reuse Slides** pane, click the slide that you want to insert.

5. If necessary, click the other slides to insert them into the presentation.

Procedure Reference: Insert an Outline

To insert an outline in a presentation:

1. Select the **Home** tab, and in the **Slides** group, from the **New Slide** drop-down list, select **Slides from Outline.**

2. In the **Insert Outline** dialog box, navigate to the desired location and select the desired file.

3. Click **Insert** to insert the outline as slides in the presentation.

ACTIVITY 2-5
Adding New Slides to a Presentation

Data Files:

C:\084592Data\Creating a Basic Presentation\My OGC Properties.pptx

Before You Begin:
The My OGC Properties.pptx file is open.

Scenario:
You want to proceed with the creation of your presentation by adding new slides to it. Your colleague has also suggested that you could use some of the slides from an older presentation that he had prepared a few months back.

---

1. Reuse the **Title and Content** slide.

    a. On the **Home** tab, in the **Slides** group, from the **New Slide** drop-down list, select **Title and Content.**

    b. In the **Click to add title** text placeholder, click and type *Income* to add a title to the slide.

---

2. Insert slides from another presentation.

    a. On the **Home** tab, in the **Slides** group, from the **New Slide** drop-down list, select **Reuse Slides.**

    b. In the **Reuse Slides** pane, from the **Browse** drop-down list, select **Browse File.**

    c. In the **Browse** dialog box, navigate to the C:\084592Data\Creating a Basic Presentation folder.

    d. Select **My OGC Financial Information.pptx** and click **Open.**

    e. In the **Reuse Slides** pane, click the slide with the title "Introduction."

    f. Click the slide with the title "Agenda" and then click the slide with the title "Highlights of the Previous Year" to insert both slides.

    g. Close the **Reuse Slides** pane.

---

3. Change the layout of a slide.

    a. Select the **Home** tab, and in the **Slides** group, click **Layout,** and from the displayed gallery, select the **Title Only** layout.

    b. Save the presentation.

TOPIC F
Arrange Slides

You added slides to a presentation. Once you create the slides for a presentation, you may want to ensure that the slides are presented in a desired sequence. In this topic, you will arrange the slides in a presentation.

When creating a presentation, you attempt to present the information in the best sequence so as to create the biggest impact. Even if you have all the information, if the slides are not sequenced correctly, it may ruin the presentation because the flow of information may be inappropriate. By understanding how to arrange slides, you can create slides without being concerned about the flow of information and rearrange the slides to suit your requirement.

How to Arrange Slides

Procedure Reference: Arrange Slides by Using the Slide Sorter View

To arrange slides by using the Slide Sorter view:

1. On the **View** tab, in the **Presentation Views** group, click **Slide Sorter.**
2. Select the slides to be rearranged.
3. Rearrange the slides.
    -   Arrange the slides by using the drag-and-drop method.
        -   Click and drag the slide to the desired location.
        -   Hold down **Ctrl** and click and drag the slide to the desired location to copy it.
    -   Arrange the slides using the cut, copy, and paste method.
        a. Cut or copy a slide.
        b. Navigate to the desired location where you want the slide to appear.
        c. Paste the slide.
4. If necessary, delete a slide.
    -   Right-click the desired slide, and from the displayed menu, choose **Delete Slide** or;
    -   Select the desired slide and press **Delete.**

 To delete multiple slides, you first need to select multiple slides before you delete them.

5. If necessary, right-click and choose **Hide Slide** to hide a slide.

Hiding Slides

Depending on the audience for your presentation, you might want to hide certain slides, but have them available as part of the presentation. By hiding slides, you can ensure that certain slides do not appear during a slide show.

Procedure Reference: Arrange Slides in the Normal View

To arrange slides in the Normal view:

1. On the **View** tab, in the **Presentation Views** group, click **Normal.**

2. In the left pane, on the **Slides** tab, select a slide.

3. Arrange the slide.

- Cut and paste the slide in the desired location to move it.
- Copy and paste the slide in the desired location to make a copy of it.
- Delete the slide.
- Hide the slide.

ACTIVITY 2-6
Arranging Slides in a Presentation

Before You Begin:
The My OGC Properties.pptx file is open.

Scenario:
You have added content to the slides in your presentation from another presentation. However, you notice that though the content is relevant to the presentation that you are developing, the slides are not arranged in a sequence. So, you decide to rearrange the slides based on the relevance of the content.

1. Move the Introduction slide to position it as the second slide in the Normal view.

    a. In the left pane, on the **Slides** tab, select slide 3.

    b. On the **Home** tab, in the **Clipboard** group, click the **Cut** button.

    c. In the left pane, on the **Slides** tab, click between slides 1 and 2.

    d. Observe that the insertion point appears between slides 1 and 2, and on the **Home** tab, in the **Clipboard** group, and click **Paste**.

2. Rearrange the Agenda and Highlights of the Previous Year slides in the Slide Sorter view.

    a. Select the **View** tab, and in the **Presentation Views** group, click **Slide Sorter.**

      b.   In the Slide Sorter view, click and drag slide 4 to place it before slide 3.

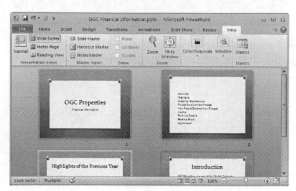

      c.   Observe that the Agenda slide is now slide 3.

      d.   On the **View** tab, in the **Presentation Views** group, click **Normal.**

      e.   Save the presentation.

TOPIC G
Work with Themes

You arranged the slides in a presentation. After ensuring that the slides are displayed in the correct order, you may want to ensure the consistent appearance of the slides in the presentation. In this topic, you will work with themes.

Imagine a presentation where every slide has a different color scheme and font style. With each slide, the audience may have to adjust their expectations and refocus their attention. By applying a consistent theme to a presentation, you can create professional presentations that are uniform in their look and feel so as not to distract your audience from the content being presented.

Themes

Definition:

A *theme* is a combination of colors, fonts, and graphics that provides a consistent visual look and feel to a presentation. Themes determine the background color of a slide as well as the colors of text, tables, or any other components in a presentation. Themes also define the fonts and the position of text placeholders. You can choose to apply a theme either to all slides or to only selected slides in a presentation.

Example:

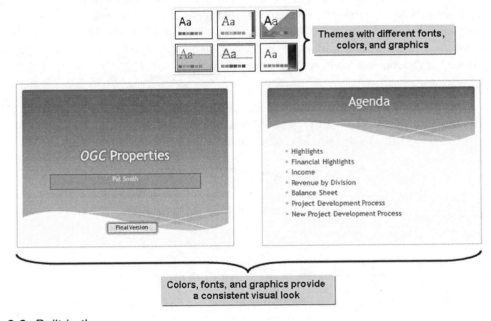

Figure 2-9: Built-in themes.

Theme Components

A theme consists of three formatting components: theme colors, theme fonts, and theme effects. After applying a predefined theme to a presentation, you can modify the individual theme components to suit your requirements.

Theme Component	Description
Colors	Colors that can be applied to theme elements. The **Colors** drop-down list in the **Themes** group enables you to customize colors in a chosen theme to suit your requirements.
Fonts	Fonts that can be applied to text on slides to which a theme is applied. The **Fonts** drop-down list in the **Themes** group enables you to select fonts that are used in a presentation theme. A presentation theme uses one font for the title and another for the body text.
Effects	Effects that can be applied to themes. The **Effects** drop-down list in the **Themes** group provides several effects that you can apply to themes.

Background Styles

A *background style* is the color and *texture* that is applied to the background of a slide. Background styles are derived from theme colors and background intensities in a chosen presentation theme. When a presentation theme is changed, the background styles are also updated to match the new theme colors and background. You can customize and modify the background styles to suit your requirements. You can also choose to have *gradient effects,* pictures, or texture variations as a slide background.

Hide Background Graphics

By checking the **Hide Background Graphics** check box, you can hide the background style of the theme that you applied to a slide. The **Hide Background Graphics** check box can be accessed on the **Design** tab in the **Background** group.

Options Available in the Format Background Dialog Box

Options to specify the appearance of slide backgrounds are available in the **Format Background** dialog box. These options are available on four separate tabs.

Tab	Description
Fill	Contains options for adding a gradient, texture, picture fill or pattern fill to a slide background. In the **Fill Color** section, you can choose a color and adjust the transparency of the fill color.
Picture Corrections	Provides options to adjust the sharpness, brightness, and contrast of a picture that is used as a background. The **Reset** button can be used to restore the default settings for brightness and contrast.
Picture Color	Provides options to select the color saturation and color tone in a background. In the **Recolor** section, you can select a preset recolor option from the **Preset** drop-down list.

Tab	Description
Artistic Effects	Provides various artistic effect options from which you can select a desired effect.

How to Work with Themes

Procedure Reference: Apply a Theme

To apply a theme:

1. On the Ribbon, select the **Design** tab.
2. Apply a theme.
    *   In the **Themes** group, select a theme or;
    *   In the **Themes** group, click the **More** button and from the displayed gallery, select a theme.
3. Click outside the gallery to close it.

Procedure Reference: Create a Custom Color Theme

To create a custom color theme:

1. On the **Design** tab, in the **Themes** group, click the **Colors** drop-down arrow, and from the displayed gallery, select **Create New Theme Colors.**
2. In the **Create New Theme Colors** dialog box, in the **Theme Colors** section, set the color options.
3. In the **Sample** section, preview the custom color theme.
4. In the **Name** text box, type a name for the custom color theme.

 To change a presentation back to its original theme, click the **Reset** button that is located in the **Create New Theme Colors** dialog box.

Procedure Reference: Create a Custom Font Theme

To create a custom font theme:

1. On the **Design** tab, in the **Themes** group, click the **Fonts** drop-down arrow, and from the displayed gallery, select **Create New Theme Fonts.**
2. In the **Create New Theme Fonts** dialog box, from the **Heading Font** drop-down list, select a font type for the slide titles.
3. From the **Body Font** drop-down list, select a font type for the slide body content.
4. In the **Sample** section, preview the custom font theme.
5. In the **Name** text box, type a name for the custom font theme.

Procedure Reference: Modify an Existing Theme

To modify an existing theme:

1. On the Ribbon, select the **Design** tab.

2. Modify an existing theme element by using the options in the **Themes** group.

    ●   Click the **Colors** drop-down arrow, and from the displayed gallery, select a color theme.

    ●   Click the **Font** drop-down arrow, and from the displayed gallery, select a font theme.

    ●   Click the **Effects** drop-down arrow, and from the displayed gallery, select an effect theme.

3. Preview the theme.

 When you create custom themes, they are stored in the gallery for future use.

Procedure Reference: Apply a Background Style

To apply a background style:

1. On the **Design** tab, in the **Background** group, click the **Background Styles** drop-down arrow, and from the displayed gallery, select a background style.

2. If necessary, on the **Design** tab, in the **Background** group, check the **Hide Background Graphics** check box to hide any background graphic from appearing on the slide.

ACTIVITY 2-7
Applying a Theme and Background Style to a Presentation

Before You Begin:
The My OGC Properties.pptx file is open.

Scenario:
The presentation that you are working on has slides with a white background color. You want to make the background of the presentation more colorful. Also, you want your presentation to have a consistent and professional look with a uniform theme throughout.

---

1. Apply the **Waveform** theme to the presentation.

    a. Select the **Design** tab, and in the **Themes** group, click the **More** button to display a gallery.

    b. From the displayed gallery, in the **Built-In** section, scroll down, and select the **Waveform** theme, which is the last theme in the last row of the section.

---

2. Modify the font and background for the theme.

    a. In the left pane, on the **Slides** tab, select Slide 1.

    b. On the **Design** tab, in the **Themes** group, click the **Fonts** drop-down arrow, and from the displayed gallery, select **Office Classic 2** to apply the theme for the titles and text in all the slides.

    c. On the **Design** tab, in the **Background** group, from the **Background Styles** drop-down list, select **Style 10,** which is the second style in the third row.

    d. Save the presentation.

    e. Close the file.

Lesson 2 Follow-up

In this lesson, you created a basic presentation. With this knowledge, you can create a framework that you can use to build a complex presentation.

1. **Do you have a preference for creating presentations from scratch with blank slides, or using existing templates? Why?**

2. **Which PowerPoint feature will you find the most useful while creating a presentation with text alone?**

3 Formatting Text on Slides

Lesson Time: 45 minutes

Lesson Objectives:

In this lesson, you will format text on slides.

You will:

- Apply character formats.
- Format paragraphs.

Introduction

You created a basic presentation with text content. You now want to enhance the appearance of text and emphasize key information. In this lesson, you will format text on slides.

Text without any kind of formatting will look the same and may fail to emphasize the importance of the content. By formatting text, you can not only add emphasis and visual appeal, but also make it easier to read. Using different character styles and formats, you can quickly format text, thus avoiding the laborious task of customizing the appearance of text.

TOPIC A
Apply Character Formats

You added text to slides. You may now want to enhance the appearance of text by modifying its properties. In this topic, you will apply character formats to text in a presentation.

When preparing a business presentation for your clients, you have to ensure that the presentation keeps the audience engrossed. In addition, you have to make sure that the audience do not lose out on any important information presented on the slides. PowerPoint 2010, with its various options to customize font colors, sizes, and styles, allows you to make the slides attractive to ensure that your audience are captivated by the information in your presentation.

Character Formats

Character formats is a set of formatting characteristics or a group of attributes that you can apply to text on a slide to modify the appearance of text. PowerPoint allows you to set various character formatting options such as the font face, size, and color by using the **Font** dialog box, or in the **Font** group on the **Home** tab.

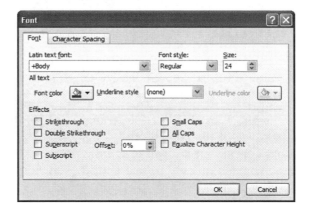

Figure 3-1: The Font dialog box.

WordArt Styles

WordArt styles are predefined text effects that can be applied to text on a slide. They are displayed as thumbnails in the **WordArt Styles** group on the **Format** contextual tab. These styles can be applied either to a selection of text or to all text within a shape on a slide. By placing the mouse pointer over a thumbnail, you can see a live preview of how the selected text will look if the style is applied. You can also use other text style options, such as **Text Fill, Text Outline,** and **Text Effects,** to make text look colorful and attractive.

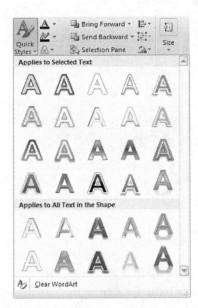

Figure 3-2: *Predefined text effects that can be applied to text on a slide.*

The Font Dialog Box

The **Font** dialog box provides you with advanced text formatting options to format text on a slide.

Option	Allows You To
The **Latin text font** drop-down list	Select a font type, such as Times New Roman or Arial.
The **Font style** drop-down list	Select a font style, such as **Regular, Italic, Bold,** and **Bold Italic.**
The **Size** spin box	Set a size for the font. You can increase or decrease the font size.
The **Font color** drop-down list	Select a font color. You can also choose from a wide spectrum of colors by using the **More Colors** option.
The **Underline style** drop-down list	Select an underline style for the text.
The **Underline color** drop-down list	Select a color for the underline.
The **Effects** section	Select font effects, such as **Strikethrough, Double Strikethrough, Superscript, Small Caps, All Caps,** and **Equalize Character Height.**

Serif vs. Sans-Serif Fonts

In typography, serifs are semi-structural details at the ends of some of the strokes that make up letters and symbols. Typefaces that have serifs are called serif typefaces, for example Times New Roman. Typefaces without serifs are called sans-serif, for example Arial or Verdana.

The Format Painter

The *Format Painter* in the **Clipboard** group on the **Home** tab provides you with an easy way to copy only the formatting applied to text instead of copying the text as a whole. The Format Painter works similar to a paintbrush, and can be used to format changes to content or to copy a color scheme from one slide to another.

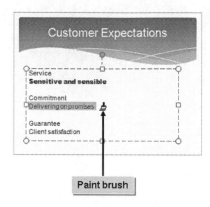

Figure 3-3: *The Format Painter used to copy formatting.*

The Replace Fonts Option

Using the **Replace Fonts** option, you can easily change the font applied to text in a presentation to another font. You can access this option from the **Replace** drop-down list in the **Editing** group on the **Home** tab. You need to specify the current font and the font with which to replace in the **Replace** and **With** drop-down lists, respectively.

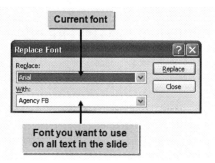

Figure 3-4: *The Replace Font dialog box.*

How to Apply Character Formats

Procedure Reference: Apply Character Formats

To apply character formats:

1. Select the desired text.
2. Apply the desired font effects.
   - On the **Home** tab, in the **Font** group, set the desired options or;
   - On the **Home** tab, in the **Font** group, click the **Font** dialog box launcher to open the **Font** dialog box.
     a. In the **Font** dialog box, set the desired options.
     b. Click **OK.**

Procedure Reference: Apply Quick Styles to Text

To apply Quick Styles to text:

1. Select the text.
2. On the **Home** tab, in the **Drawing** group, from the **Quick Styles** drop-down list, select a text style.

Applying Styles to Shapes

You can also apply a text style for the text embedded in a shape by selecting the shape and selecting a style from the **Shape Styles** group on the **Format** contextual tab.

Procedure Reference: Replace a Font in a Presentation

To replace a font in a presentation:

1. On the **Home** tab, in the **Editing** group, from the **Replace** drop-down list, select **Replace Fonts.**
2. In the **Replace Font** dialog box, from the **Replace** drop-down list, select the font to be replaced.
3. From the **With** drop-down list, select a font that will replace the font listed in the **Replace** drop-down list.
4. Click **Replace.**

Procedure Reference: Format Text by Using the Format Painter

To format text by using the Format Painter:

1. Select the text that has the format you want to copy.
2. Copy the format of the selected text.
   - On the **Home** tab, in the **Clipboard** group, click the **Format Painter** button to copy the formatting or;
   - Double-click the **Format Painter** button to copy the formatting to apply it to multiple instances of text.
3. When the mouse pointer changes to a paint brush, click and drag the mouse pointer over the text to which you want to apply the text formatting.
4. Click outside the slide to deactivate the **Format Painter** button.

ACTIVITY 3-1
Applying Character Formatting to Text on Slides

Data Files:

C:\084592Data\Formatting Text on Slides\OGC Properties.pptx

Scenario:

While reviewing the PowerPoint presentation that you created, you realize that you can make it look better by formatting text. You also want to enhance the appearance of titles on the sixth and eighth slides.

1. Apply bold formatting to the word "Service."

    a. Navigate to the C:\084592Data\Formatting Text on Slides folder and open the OGC Properties.pptx file.

    b. In the left pane, on the **Slides** tab, scroll down and select slide 6.

    c. On the slide, double-click the word "Service" to select it.

    d. Select the **Home** tab, and in the **Font** group, click the **Bold** button. [B]

2. Use the Mini toolbar to bold format the words "Commitment" and "Guarantee."

    a. Double-click the word "Commitment," which is below the word "Sensitive and sensible," to select it.

    b. Observe that the Mini toolbar is displayed above the selection.

    c. Move the mouse pointer over the Mini toolbar and click the **Bold** button.

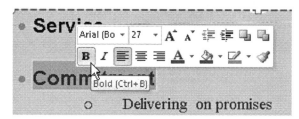

    d. Observe that the word "Commitment" is displayed with bold formatting applied to it.

    e. Similarly, apply bold formatting to the word "Guarantee," which is below the text "Delivering on promises."

3. Apply the Verdana font to the bullet points.

    a. Triple-click on the word "sensible" to select the text "Sensitive and sensible," which is below the word "Service."

b. On the **Home** tab, in the **Font** group, in the **Font** drop-down list, scroll down and select **Verdana** to change the font type.

> 𝕋 Tw Cen MT Condensed
>
> 𝕋 **Tw Cen MT Condensed Extra Bold**
>
> 𝕋 Verdana

c. In the **Clipboard** group, double-click the **Format Painter** button. 🖌

d. Observe that the mouse pointer has changed to a paintbrush/insertion point combination.

e. Click and drag the mouse pointer over the text "Delivering on promises," which is below the word "Commitment," to apply the copied text formatting.

> 🖌]Delivering on promises

f. Similarly, click and drag the mouse pointer over the text "Client satisfaction," which is below the text "Guarantee," to apply the same formatting.

g. On the **Home** tab, in the **Clipboard** group, click the **Format Painter** button to deactivate the Format Painter.

4. Apply character styles to the text in the presentation.

a. In the left pane, on the **Slides** tab, select slide 8, and on the slide, triple-click the text "Expenditures down by 10%," which is just below the text "Sales up in Q2 by 15%."

b. On the **Home** tab, in the **Font** group, click the **Font** dialog box launcher.

c. In the **Font** dialog box, on the **Font** tab, in the **All text** section, from the **Underline style** drop-down list, select the third option to apply the doubleline underline style.

d. In the **All text** section, from the **Underline color** gallery, in the **Standard Colors** section, select **Blue,** which is the third color from the right.

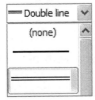

e. In the **Effects** section, check the **Small Caps** check box and click **OK.**

f. Observe that the character styles are applied to the text "Expenditures down by 10%"

g. Deselect the text.

h. Save the file as ***My OGC Properties***

TOPIC B
Format Paragraphs

You formatted text in a presentation to make it look more appealing. You may also need to improve its readability by formatting paragraphs of text. In this topic, you will format paragraphs of textual content in presentations.

Text content, if not presented effectively, will fail to convey the intended message to an audience. Imagine a book that fails to differentiate the title from other sections of the content. Similarly, a presentation without any formatting of paragraph text will fail to attract the users' attention and interest. Applying paragraph formats and typography effects enhances the readability of the content and allows you to stress on the importance of certain portions of text.

Bulleted Lists

Bulleted lists are used to organize and display text in a structured format. A bulleted list is a list of items, each beginning with a bullet. You can choose to use a bulleted list when the sequence of items in a list does not have to follow a linear pattern. PowerPoint not only enables you to add bullets, but also provides a variety of options that you can use to format the bullets. You can choose from a variety of bullet types that are available in PowerPoint. The **Increase List Level** and **Decrease List Level** options help you increase or decrease the space between the bullet and the margins of the text placeholder to create sublevels of bulleted lists.

Figure 3-5: Options to format a bulleted list.

The **Bulleted** tab in the **Bullets and Numbering** dialog box provides you with options to customize the appearance of bullets.

Option	Enables You To
Shape	Choose from **Filled Round, Hollow Round, Filled Square, Hollow Square, Star, Arrow,** and **Checkmark** bullet types.
Size	Set the bullet size as a percentage of the text size.
Color	Change the color of a bullet.
Picture	Use a bullet graphic from the **Picture Bullet** dialog box or import an image as a bullet graphic.
Customize	Use a symbol as a bullet.

Numbered Lists

In addition to bulleted lists, PowerPoint allows you to format text by using numbered lists. You can choose the Arabic or the Roman numbering system to number the items in a list. You can also use letters of the alphabet to number the items in a list.

Figure 3-6: Options to format a numbered list.

The **Numbered** tab in the **Bullets and Numbering** dialog box provides you with options to specify the number system and the appearance of numbering for list items.

Number Option	Enables You To
Number System	Set the numbering system as numeric, roman, or alphabetic.
Size	Set the font size of the numbers as a percentage of the size of the list text.
Color	Change the font color of only the numbers, but not the font color of the text.
Start at	Specify the initial value of the number or letter with which the numbering of a list begins.

Text Alignment Options

The *text alignment* options in PowerPoint enable you to align the text inside a text box in relation to the margins of the text box.

Alignment Option	Result
Align Text Left	The left edge of every line of text is aligned to the left margin of the text box.
Center	The center of every line of text is aligned to the center of the text box.
Align Text Right	The right edge of every line of text is aligned to the right margin of the text box.
Justify	The left and right edges of every line of text are aligned to the left and right margins of the text box, respectively.

Spacing Options

Spacing refers to the vertical distance between lines or paragraphs of text. PowerPoint provides you with three spacing options.

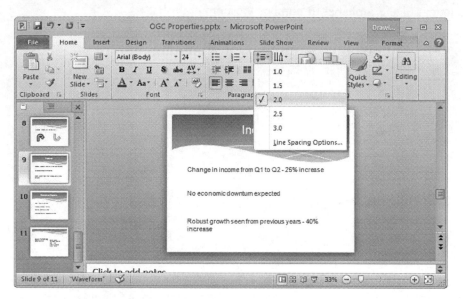

Figure 3-7: *Spacing options in PowerPoint.*

Spacing Option	Enables You To
Line Spacing	Change the spacing between lines of text in a paragraph.
Before	Change the spacing between paragraphs by altering the space before a paragraph.
After	Change the spacing between paragraphs by altering the space after a paragraph.

Rulers

PowerPoint provides you with the vertical and horizontal rulers that allow you to accurately position objects on a slide. The horizontal and vertical rulers are located at the top and left edges of the slide pane, respectively. Each ruler consists of marked increments that help you position slide objects. The margins and indents inside the text placeholders can be controlled by adjusting their positions on the rulers.

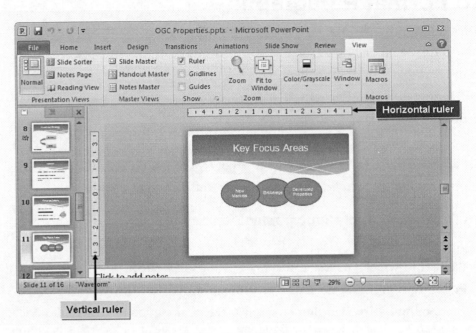

Figure 3-8: Rulers in the PowerPoint application window.

Typography Effects

In addition to the standard text formatting options, PowerPoint 2010 provides you with *typography effects* that can be used to apply additional formatting to text.

Typography Effect	Allows You To
Text Direction	Orient text in different directions, such as vertical, stacked, horizontal, or rotated.
Wrap Text In Shape	Place text within a shape so that the lines of text are aligned to the edges of the shape.
Columns	Split a text box into two or more columns. You can also define the spacing between columns.
Autofit	Resize shape to fit text by increasing the size of the shape vertically so that the text fits inside it.

The Clear All Formatting Button

The *Clear All Formatting* button enables you to remove all formatting applied to text and restore text to its default format.

How to Format Paragraphs

Procedure Reference: Modify Text Alignment and Orientation

To modify text alignment and orientation:

1. Select the text that you want to align.
2. On the **Home** tab, in the **Paragraph** group, set the alignment option.
   - Click the **Align Text Left** button to align text to the left.
   - Click the **Center** button to center text.
   - Click the **Align Text Right** button to align text to the right.
   - Click the **Justify** button to align text to the left and right margins.

Procedure Reference: Apply Typography Effects

To apply typography effects:

1. Select the text to which you want to apply a typography effect.
2. In the **Paragraph** group, select suitable typography effects.
   - From the **Text Direction** drop-down list, select an option to change the orientation of the text to vertical, stacked, or horizontal, or to rotate it in a certain direction.
   - From the **Text Direction** drop-down list, select **More Options,** and in the **Format Text Effects** dialog box, click the **Columns** button to split the text into two or more columns.

Procedure Reference: Set the Line Spacing

To set the line spacing:

1. Position the insertion point in a paragraph or select the paragraph to which you want to apply line spacing.
2. On the **Drawing Tools** tab, on the **Format** contextual tab, in the **Paragraph** group, click **Line Spacing,** and from the drop-down list, select the desired spacing option.

Procedure Reference: Change the Indents

To change the indents:

1. Select the text that you want to indent.
2. On the **View** tab, in the **Show** group, check the **Ruler** check box to display the ruler.
3. Indent text by using the options in the **Paragraph** group.
   - On the **Home** tab, in the **Paragraph** group, click the **Increase List Level** button to increase the indent level.
   - On the **Home** tab, in the **Paragraph** group, click the **Decrease List Level** button to decrease the indent level.
4. If necessary, on the **View** tab, in the **Show** group, check the **Ruler** check box to hide the ruler.

Procedure Reference: Adjust Text Box Margins

To adjust text box margins:

1. Select the text box for which you want to adjust the margins.
2. Display the **Format Shape** dialog box.
3. In the **Format Shape** dialog box, select the **Text box** tab.

4. In the **Internal Margin** section, set the desired settings for the text box margins.

Procedure Reference: Create a Bulleted or Numbered List

To create a bulleted or numbered list:

1. Position the insertion point where you want to start a list.

2. Create a list.

    - Specify a bullet format.

        ■ On the **Home** tab, in the **Paragraph** group, click the **Bullets** button or;

        ■ On the **Home** tab, in the **Paragraph** group, click the **Bullets** drop-down arrow, and from the displayed list, select the desired bullet.

    - Specify a numbering format.

        ■ On the **Home** tab, in the **Paragraph** group, click the **Numbering** button or;

        ■ On the **Home** tab, in the **Paragraph** group, click the **Numbering** drop-down arrow, and from the displayed list, select the desired numbering format.

Procedure Reference: Transform Paragraphs into Lists

To transform paragraphs into lists:

1. Select the paragraphs that will be included in the list.

2. Specify a bullet or numbering format to create a list.

Procedure Reference: Format Bullets or Numbers of Lists

To format bullets or numbers of lists:

1. Select a list.

2. Display the **Bullets and Numbering** dialog box.

    - On the **Home** tab, in the **Paragraph** group, from the **Bullets** drop-down list, select **Bullets and Numbering** or;

    - On the **Home** tab, in the **Paragraph** group, from the **Numbering** drop-down list, select **Bullets and Numbering.**

3. Select the desired format.

    - From the **Color** drop-down list, select a color.

    - In the **Size** text box, enter a value.

4. Click **OK** to apply the selected format.

ACTIVITY 3-2
Applying Paragraph Formats to Text

Before You Begin:
The My OGC Properties.pptx file is open.

Scenario:
While reviewing the presentation that you just created, you realize that you can enhance the text content on a few slides. You want to format paragraphs of text so that the text in the presentation is easily readable to the audience.

---

1. Display text in two columns.

   a. In the left pane, on the **Slides** tab, scroll up and select slide 3.

   b. On the slide, click before the letter "A" in the text "About Us" and press **Ctrl+A** to select all the text.

   c. On the **Home** tab, in the **Paragraph** group, from the **Columns** drop-down list, select **Two Columns.**

   d. Observe that the text on the slide is split across two columns and the space between the columns is insufficient.

   e. From the **Columns** drop-down list, select **More Columns.**

   f. In the **Columns** dialog box, in the **Spacing** text box, triple-click and type *0.5* and then click **OK.**

   g. Deselect the text.

   h. Observe that the text is now displayed with adequate space between the two columns.

---

2. Format text as a bulleted list.

   a. In the left pane, on the **Slides** tab, select slide 6.

   b. Click before the letter "S" in the word "Service" and press **Ctrl+A** to select all the text.

   c. On the **Home** tab, in the **Paragraph** group, click the **Bullets** button.

   d. Deselect the text.

---

e.   Observe that the text on the slide appears as a bulleted list.

3.   Change the line spacing on the "About Us" slide.

   a.   In the left pane, on the **Slides** tab, scroll up, select slide 4, and click before the letter "O" in the text "OGC Properties" to display the text placeholder.

   b.   On the **Home** tab, in the **Paragraph** group, from the **Line Spacing** drop-down list, select **1.5** to change the spacing.

4.   Indent the bulleted list.

   a.   In the left pane, on the **Slides** tab, select slide 6 and click before the letter "S" in the word "Service" to display the text placeholder.

   b.   Triple-click to select the text "Sensitive and Sensible."

   c.   On the **Home** tab, in the **Paragraph** group, click the **Increase list level** button.

   d.   Similarly, indent the text "Delivering on promises" and "Client satisfaction." This will be done for you.

5.   Change the bullet style for the indented items.

   a.   Click before the word "Sensitive" in the bulleted item "Sensitive and sensible."

   b.   On the **Home** tab, and in the **Paragraph** group, from the **Bullets** gallery, select **Filled Round Bullets,** which is the second bullet option in the first row.

   c.   On the **Home** tab, in the **Paragraph** group, from the **Bullets** gallery, select **Bullets and Numbering** to launch the **Bullets and Numbering** dialog box.

   d.   On the **Bulleted** tab, select **Color,** and from the displayed gallery, in the **Standard Colors** section, select **Orange,** which is the third color from the left, and click **OK.**

   e.   Similarly, apply the same bullet style and color to the text "Delivering on promises" and "Client satisfaction."

   f.   Save and close the presentation.

Lesson 3 Follow-up

In this lesson, you formatted text on slides. This skill facilitates adding emphasis to specific areas of a slide and better readability of slides.

1. **What type of character formatting do you think you will use often in your presentations?**

2. **What PowerPoint options do you like to use to format text on slides to enhance text appearance?**

4 | Adding Graphical Objects to a Presentation

Lesson Time: 1 hour(s)

Lesson Objectives:

In this lesson, you will add graphical objects to a presentation.

You will:

- Insert images into a presentation.
- Add shapes.
- Add visual styles to the text in a presentation.

Introduction

You formatted text in a presentation. Adding graphical objects to slides to complement the text displayed on a slide will reinforce the message and engage the audience. In this lesson, you will add graphical objects to a presentation.

Adding graphical objects to a presentation not only help you in effectively illustrating difficult concepts, but also in making the audience understand the text in the presentation. By emphasizing key points in text through appropriate graphical elements, you can generate and sustain the audience's interest in the presentation.

TOPIC A
Insert Images into a Presentation

You formatted paragraphs and lists in a presentation. You may need to use a combination of text and graphics in your presentations to engage the audience. In this topic, you will add images to a presentation.

A presentation containing only textual content is not an effective way to express an idea. A picture is worth a thousand words and will help you communicate even complicated concepts effectively. Using images in presentations helps you draw the attention of the audience to the key points of discussion and also engages them to focus on just the relevant details.

Clip Art

Definition:

Clip art is a graphical image in a digital format that you can insert into a presentation. The **Clip Art** gallery is a repository of several kinds of clip art images. In addition, the gallery contains photographs, movies, and sound clippings. You can search for and locate a specific graphical element quickly in the **Clip Art** gallery by using keywords. If you are unable to locate a specific clip from the gallery, then you can search the Microsoft website, where thousands of clip art are available.

Example:

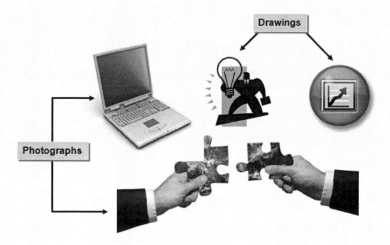

Figure 4-1: Clip art images that can be inserted into a presentation.

The Clip Art Pane

The *Clip Art pane* allows you to search for a clip art by typing a keyword that best describes the clip art you are searching for, or select a category to search from the **Results should be** drop-down list.

The Photo Album Feature

The *Photo Album* feature is used to insert photographs and display them in a presentation as a photo album. You can enhance a photo album by adding transitions, colorful backgrounds, layouts, captions, and themes to the slides in the presentation. A photo album can be shared with other users as an attachment, published on the web, or printed. You can use the **Photo Album** dialog box to insert pictures into an album, add captions to pictures, convert all pictures as black and white, modify the album layout, add frames to photos, rotate photos, or set the brightness and contrast.

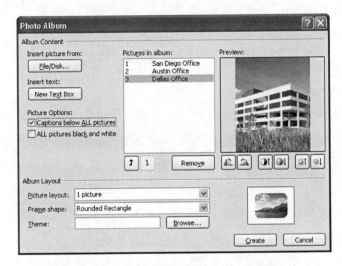

Figure 4-2: Options to enhance photos in the Photo Album dialog box.

The Screenshot Tool

The screenshot tool in PowerPoint lets you capture an image of your computer's screen. Accessed by clicking the **Screenshot** button in the **Images** group on the **Insert** tab, this feature allows you to capture the complete screen, an active window, or a portion of the screen by using a marquee selection tool.

Figure 4-3: The Screenshot tool displaying active windows.

How to Insert Images into a Presentation

Procedure Reference: Insert a Screenshot into a Presentation

To insert a screenshot into a presentation:

1. Open the application that you want to capture as a screenshot.
2. Navigate to the slide in which you want to insert the screenshot.
3. On the **Insert** tab, in the **Images** group, click the **Screenshot** drop-down arrow to pre-view the window that needs to be captured.
4. Capture the screen.
   - From the **Screenshot** drop-down list, in the **Available Windows** section, select the window that needs to be captured and observe as the screenshot gets inserted in the slide.
   - Capture a portion of the screen.
     - From the **Screenshot** drop-down list, select **Screen Clipping.**
     - Use the marquee tool to select the desired portion of the screen.

Procedure Reference: Insert Clip Art

To insert clip art:

1. Navigate to the slide in which you want to insert clip art.
2. Select the **Insert** tab, and in the **Images** group, click **Clip Art.**
3. In the **Clip Art** task pane, search for the desired image.
   - In the **Search for** text box, type a search word that best describes the image.
   - From the **Results should be** drop-down list, select a category to search in.
4. If necessary, in the **Microsoft Clip Organizer** dialog box, click **Yes** to include additional clip art images from Microsoft Office Online.
5. Click **Go.**
6. From the displayed results, select the clip art that you want to insert.

Procedure Reference: Insert a Picture

To insert a picture:

1. Navigate to the slide in which you want to insert a picture.
2. On the **Insert** tab, in the **Images** group, click **Picture.**
3. In the **Insert Picture** dialog box, navigate to the folder that contains the picture.
4. Insert the picture.
   - Double-click the file name of the picture to insert it in the presentation or;
   - Select the picture and click **Insert.**

Procedure Reference: Create a Photo Album

To create a photo album:

1. On the **Insert** tab, in the **Images** group, click the **Photo Album** button.
2. In the **Photo Album** dialog box, in the **Insert picture from** section, click **File/Disk.**
3. In the **Insert New Pictures** dialog box, navigate to the desired folder, select the desired image, and click **Insert.**

4. If necessary, in the **Insert New Pictures** dialog box, in the **Album Layout** section, from the **Picture Layout** drop-down list, select the desired layout option.

5. Similarly, insert the rest of the pictures in the album.

6. If necessary, click **New Text Box** to add a text slide.

7. If necessary, rearrange the order of the pictures in the album.

   a. In the **Pictures in album** section, select the desired picture or text box.

   b. Rearrange the order.

      • Click the **Up** button to move the selected picture or text box up.

      • Click the **Down** button to move the selected picture or text box down.

      • Click **Remove** to remove the selected picture or text box from the photo album.

8. If necessary, in the **Album Layout** section, specify the options to modify the album layout.

   • From the **Picture layout** drop-down list, select a layout option or;

   • From the **Frame shape** drop-down list, select a frame shape.

   • Select the desired theme.

      a. In the **Theme** section, click **Browse.**

      b. In the **Choose Theme** dialog box, navigate to the desired folder.

      c. Select a theme and click **Select.**

9. If necessary, in the **Picture Options** section, specify the picture options.

   • Check the **Captions below ALL pictures** check box to display a caption text below the picture.

   • Check the **ALL pictures black and white** check box to convert pictures into black and white.

10. If necessary, below the **Preview** section, set the desired options to adjust the image.

    • Click the Rotate left button to rotate the image counter clockwise.

    • Click the Rotate right button to rotate the image clockwise.

    • Click the Increase contrast button to increase the contrast.

    • Click the Decrease contrast button to decrease the contrast.

    • Click the Increase brightness button to increase the brightness.

    • Click the Decrease brightness button to decrease the brightness.

11. Click **Create** to create the photo album.

ACTIVITY 4-1

Inserting Clip Art and Pictures into a Presentation

Data Files:

C:\084592Data\Adding Graphical Objects to a Presentation\OGC Properties.pptx,
C:\084592Data\Adding Graphical Objects to a Presentation\Appreciation.docx, C:\084592Data\
Adding Graphical Objects to a Presentation\Jane Doe.png

Before You Begin:

Open Microsoft Office Word 2010, navigate to the C:\084592Data\Adding Graphical Objects to
a Presentation folder, open the Appreciation.docx file, and on the **View** tab, click **One Page** to
display a complete page of the Word file.

Scenario:

Your manager received a copy of the letter of appreciation from the CEO of the company con-
gratulating the employees and has asked you to include it in your presentation. He has also
suggested that you add a slide to congratulate the employees who have been recognized for
their efforts during the previous year. To complement the text in the presentation, you want to
include the pictures of the employees in the slides. While going through the slides, you also
feel that using images in the presentation will make it visually appealing.

---

1.   Insert a screenshot.

   a.   Navigate to the C:\084592Data\Adding Graphical Objects to a Presentation folder and
        open the OGC Properties.pptx file.

   b.   On the **Slides** tab, scroll down and select slide 12.

   c.   Select the **Insert** tab, and in the **Images** group, from the **Screenshot** drop-down list,
        select **Screen Clipping.**

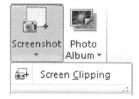

   d.   Observe that the Appreciation.docx document is displayed in gray and that the
        mouse pointer appears as a cross hair.

   e.   At the top-left corner of the page, click and drag the mouse pointer to the bottom-
        right corner of the page to capture the page as an image.

   f.   Observe that the screenshot is placed on the slide.

   g.   Click and drag the letter and place it below the Recognition title.

---

2.   Insert a business theme clip art image.

   a.   On the **Slides** tab, scroll up and select slide 10.

---

b.   On the slide, in the right placeholder, click the **Clip Art** icon.

c.   In the **Clip Art** task pane, in the **Search for** text box, click and type *board meeting* and click **Go.**

d.   Click the displayed clip art.

e.   Observe that the clip art is displayed on the slide.

f.   Close the **Clip Art** task pane.

---

3.   Insert the images of the employees you want to recognize.

a.   Select the **Insert** tab and in the **Images** group, click **Picture.**

b.   In the **Insert Picture** dialog box, navigate to the C:\084592Data\Adding Graphical Objects to a Presentation folder.

c.   Select the **Jane Doe.png** file and click **Insert.**

d.   Click and drag the image and place it in the **Click to add text** placeholder.

e.   Save the file as *My OGC Properties* in the PPTX format.

f.   Switch to the Word application.

g.   Close the Word application.

ACTIVITY 4-2
Creating a Photo Album

Data Files:

C:\084592Data\Adding Graphical Objects to a Presentation\Austin Office.png, C:\084592Data\ Adding Graphical Objects to a Presentation\San Diego Office.png, C:\084592Data\Adding Graphical Objects to a Presentation\Dallas Office.png

Before You Begin:

The My OGC Properties.pptx file is open.

Scenario:

While creating the presentation about OGC Properties, your CEO informs you that he wants to project pictures of the OGC offices that were established in different cities during the previous year. Including all the pictures into the presentation might make it lengthy. So, you decide to create a separate photo album with the images.

---

1. Select the images for the photo album.

    a. Select the **Insert** tab, and in the **Images** group, click **Photo Album.**

    b. In the **Photo Album** dialog box, in the **Insert picture from** section, click **File/Disk.**

     The Adding Graphical Objects to a Presentation folder is automatically displayed because it was used in the previous activity.

    c. Click the **Austin Office.png** file, hold down **Ctrl,** and click the **Dallas Office.png,** and **San Diego Office.png** files.

    d. Click **Insert** to insert the selected images in the photo album.

---

2. Modify the photo album.

a.   In the **Pictures in album** section, select **Austin Office** and click the Down button.

b.   In the **Album Layout** section, from the **Picture layout** drop-down list, select **1 picture** to display one picture on each slide.

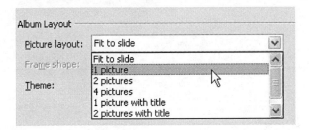

c.   From the **Frame shape** drop-down list, select **Rounded Rectangle.**

d.   In the **Picture Options** section, check the **Captions below ALL pictures** check box.

e.   Click **Create** to create the photo album.

3.   Save the presentation as a PowerPoint slide show.

a.   On the Quick Access toolbar, click **Save.**

b.   In the **Save As** dialog box, in the **File name** text box, type *OGC New Locations*

c.   In the **Save as type** drop-down list, scroll down and select **PowerPoint Show (*.ppsx).**

d.   Save and close the presentation.

4.   View the photo album as a slide show.

a.   Navigate to the C:\084592Data\Adding Graphical Objects to a Presentation folder.

b.   Double-click the **OGC New Locations.ppsx** file to open it.

c.   Observe that in the presentation, slide 1 Photo Album is displayed. Then, select the **Slide Show** tab, and in the **Start Slide Show** group, click **From Beginning.**

d.   Click the slide to view the slide with the San Diego Office image.

e.   Click the slide to view the slide with the Dallas Office image.

f.   Click the slide to view the slide with the Austin Office image.

g.   Right-click the slide and choose **End Show.**

h.   Close the OGC New Locations.ppsx presentation.

TOPIC B
Add Shapes

You added clip art and pictures to a presentation. Another way to make your presentations more appealing and visually effective is by emphasizing a particular area of a slide by adding geometric objects. In this topic, you will add shapes to a slide.

Shapes can sometimes help draw the attention of an audience to a particular area of a slide. PowerPoint provides you with several shape styles to enable you to add more visual appeal to slides. You can also add color and visual effects to shapes to further engage the audience.

Shapes

Definition:

Shapes are simple geometric objects that are built into the PowerPoint application. You can modify them and use as building blocks within a presentation. The basic component of a shape is a line that forms the outline of that shape. A shape can contain text and specific colors. You can apply a different style and color to the outline of a shape.

Example:

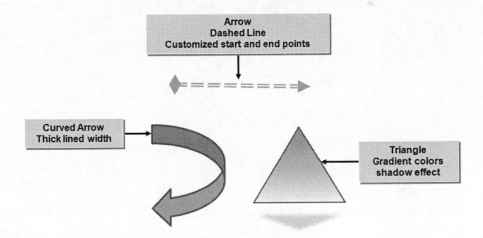

Figure 4-4: The built-in geometric objects in PowerPoint.

Shape Categories

The shapes available in PowerPoint are organized into eight categories that you can use to illustrate content on a slide.

Shape Category	Examples
Lines	Line, Double Arrow, Elbow Connector, and Elbow Arrow Connector.
Rectangles	Rectangle, Rounded Rectangle, and Snip Single Corner Rectangle.
Basic Shapes	Oval, Parallelogram, Trapezoid, Diamond, and Regular Pentagon.
Block Arrows	Right Arrow, Left Arrow, Up Arrow, and Down Arrow.

Shape Category	Examples
Equation Shapes	Plus, Minus, Multiply, Division, Equal, and Not Equal.
Flowchart	Process, Alternate Process, Decision, Data, and Display.
Stars and Banners	4-Point, 5-Point, 6-Point, and 7-Point star.
Callouts	Rectangular Callout, Rounded Rectangular Callout, Oval Callout, Cloud Callout, and Line Callout.
Action Buttons	Back, Forward, Beginning, and End.

Drawing Tools

The **Format** contextual tab of the **Drawing Tools** tool tab provides commands that enable you to insert various shapes and apply effects and styles to the shapes, as well as fill them with color. You can also change the shape of a selected drawing. The commands in the **Arrange** group enable you to arrange various shapes on a slide, align the edges of multiple selected objects, and rotate or flip the selected object to suit your requirements. You can also resize a shape after inserting it in a slide.

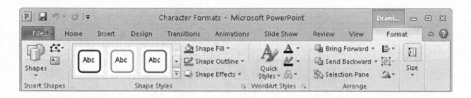

Figure 4-5: Drawing tool commands used to insert and modify shapes.

How to Add Shapes

Procedure Reference: Add Shapes to a Slide

To add shapes to a slide:

1. Navigate to the slide in which you want to add a shape.
2. If necessary, on the **View** tab, in the **Show** group, check the **Ruler** check box to view the ruler.
3. On the **Home** tab, in the **Drawing** group, click **Shape,** and from the displayed gallery, select a shape.
4. Add the required shape in the **Slide** pane.
   - In the **Slide** pane, point the cross hair mouse pointer to the top-left corner of the area where you want to draw the shape and drag diagonally down to the right to create the shape with the size you want or;
   - Click anywhere on the slide to place a default-sized shape.
5. If necessary, type text in the inserted shape.

Procedure Reference: Apply Styles to Shapes

To apply styles to shapes:

1. Select the shape to which you want to apply a style.

2.   On the **Home** tab, in the **Drawing** group, click **Quick Styles,** and from the displayed gallery, select an option.

3.   If necessary, right-click the shape and choose **Default Shape** to set the format of the current shape as the default for future shapes.

ACTIVITY 4-3
Drawing Shapes on a Slide

Before You Begin:
The My OGC Properties.pptx file is open.

Scenario:
You have added the images of the employees who have received awards in this year. As per your organization's HR guidelines on awards and recognition, you need to add the names of the award-winning employees in your presentation. While adding the names, you want to ensure that the slide looks appealing too.

1.   Add a label to the photograph.

   a.   Select the **View** tab, and in the **Show** group, check the **Ruler** check box.

   b.   Select the **Home** tab, and in the **Drawing** group, click **Shapes.**

   c.   From the **Shapes** drop-down list, in the **Rectangles** section, select **Rounded Rectangle,** which is the second shape from the left.

   d.   Above the image on the left, create a rounded rectangle shape.

   e.   In the text box, type *Jane Doe*

2.   Apply a shape style to the label.

   a.   On the **Home** tab, in the **Drawing** group, click **Quick Styles,** and from the displayed gallery, select **Subtle Effect - Blue, Accent 1,** which is the second style in the fourth row.

   b.   Save the presentation.

TOPIC C
Add Visual Styles to the Text in a Presentation

You added shapes to a presentation. There may be instances when you want the presentation text to be more eye catching and visually appealing. In this topic, you will add visual styles to the text on a slide.

To create effective presentations, you need to gauge the expectations of the audience. For example, they may require a presentation with illustrations to help them stay engaged and interested. Visual styles applied to text enhance the appearance of the content on a slide and make it stand out from the rest of the content. By manipulating the appearance of the text, you can also create a dynamic presentation, which will retain the audience's attention.

WordArt

Definition:

WordArt is a text style that you can apply to text to turn it into an editable piece of art. The **WordArt** gallery provides various built-in styles for changing plain text into shadowed, skewed, rotated, and stretched text, as well as text within predefined shapes. WordArt styles can be combined with any font to design interesting and creative graphic effects.

Example:

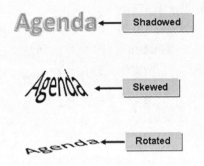

Figure 4-6: Text with WordArt styles applied.

How to Add Visual Styles to the Text in a Presentation

Procedure Reference: Convert Text to WordArt

To convert text to WordArt:

1. Select the text that you want to convert to WordArt.
2. On the **Insert** tab, in the **Text** group, click **WordArt.**
3. From the **WordArt** gallery, select the desired style.

Procedure Reference: Modify a WordArt Style

To modify a WordArt style:

1. Select the WordArt object on a slide.
2. On the **Drawing Tools** tool tab, on the **Format** contextual tab, in the **WordArt Styles** group, click the **More** button to select from a variety of preset styles.

    -   Click **Text Fill,** and from the displayed list, select a color or texture.
    -   Click **Text Outline,** and from the displayed list, select an outline color or texture.
    -   Click **Text Effects,** and from the displayed list, select a text effect.

3. If necessary, select the text in the WordArt and type the new text to update the text in the WordArt.

Procedure Reference: Change a WordArt Shape

To change a WordArt shape:

1. Select a WordArt object on a slide.
2. On the **Drawing Tools** tool tab, on the **Format** contextual tab, select the **Format** tab.
3. In the **Shape Styles** group, select one of the three styles displayed, or click the **More** button to select from a variety of shapes.

ACTIVITY 4-4
Adding WordArt to a Slide

Before You Begin:
The My OGC Properties.pptx file is open.

Scenario:
You want to enhance the appearance of the presentation title in the first slide of your presentation to impress the audience.

---

1. Apply a text style to the presentation title.

   a. In the left pane, on the **Slides** tab, scroll up and select slide 1.

   b. Triple-click the title "OGC Properties" to select it.

   c. On the **Drawing Tools** tool tab, select the **Format** contextual tab.

   d. In the **WordArt Styles** group, click the **More** button, and in the displayed gallery, in the **Applies to Selected Text** section, select the **Fill - White, Drop Shadow** WordArt style, which is the third style in the first row.

---

2. Modify the WordArt style.

   a. On the **Drawing Tools** tab, in the **WordArt Styles** group, click the **Text Outline** drop-down arrow, [icon] and in the **Theme Colors** section, select **Black,** which is the second color in the first row.

   b. In the **WordArt Styles** group, click the **Text Effects** drop-down arrow, [icon] and place the mouse pointer over the **Glow** option and from the displayed gallery, in the **Glow Variations** section, select the **Blue 5 pt glow, Accent color 2** effect, which is the second effect in the first row, to apply the effect to the text..

   c. In the **WordArt Styles** group, click the **Format Text Effects: Text Box** dialog box launcher and select the **Reflection** tab.

   d. In the **Reflection** section, click the **Presets** drop-down arrow, and from the displayed gallery, select the **Tight Reflection, touching** effect, which is placed first in the second row.

   e. Click **Close.**

   f. Save and close the My OGC Properties.pptx presentation.

Lesson 4 Follow-up

In this lesson, you added graphical objects to a presentation. By using graphical objects, you will be able to get your message across to the audience in a more concise and effective manner than by using just text.

1.   **In what situations do you expect to use clip art on a slide?**

2.   **Which shapes do you think you will use the most often in your presentations? Why?**

5 | Modifying Graphical Objects in a Presentation

Lesson Time: 45 minutes

Lesson Objectives:

In this lesson, you will modify graphical objects in a presentation.

You will:

- Edit graphical objects.
- Format graphical objects.
- Group graphical objects on a slide.
- Arrange graphical objects on a slide.
- Apply animation effects.

Introduction

You inserted graphical objects in a PowerPoint presentation. You may need to customize the appearance of these objects to suit your specific needs. In this lesson, you will modify graphical objects in a presentation.

A slide in which graphical objects are placed randomly and are of varying sizes will make the slide look cluttered. It will also distract the audience from the information you are trying to convey. By modifying the size of graphical objects and positioning them appropriately, you can gain the audience's maximum focus on just the most relevant aspects of the presentation.

TOPIC A
Edit Graphical Objects

You added graphics to a slide. After inserting graphical objects, you may need to resize or change their appearance, improve their visibility, or establish their relative importance. In this topic, you will edit graphical objects on a slide.

Graphical objects should complement the presentation content and not distract the audience from the key ideas of a presentation. If an object on a slide is too large or too small, you can resize it to improve its visibility or establish its relative importance. By editing objects on a slide to meet requirements, you can make your presentation look more impressive, apt, and neat.

Object Selection Methods

Before you can modify an object, you must select it. When an object is selected, it becomes active, and sizing handles and rotation handles appear around the object placeholder.

PowerPoint provides various methods that you can use to select objects on a slide.

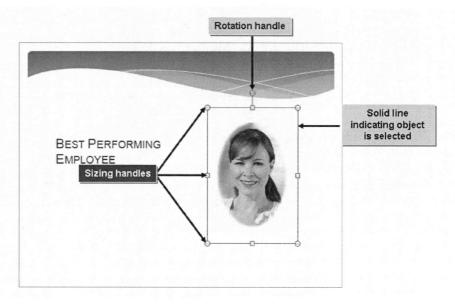

Figure 5-1: A selected object.

Selection Option	Allows You To
Select All	Select all the objects on a slide.
Select Objects	Select rectangular regions of ink strokes, shapes and text.
Selection Pane	Select several objects on a single slide. When you select items in the list in the **Selection and Visibility**pane, the corresponding objects are selected on the slide.

The Remove Background Tool

Remove Background is a tool that is used to remove backgrounds from images. If you want to include an image with transparent background in your presentation, then this tool comes in handy. Clicking the **Remove Background** button automatically selects the background of the image to give you an idea of the background area that you may want to remove. If the selected background area does not suit your requirements, then you can use the sizing handles to define the background area for removal.

Figure 5-2: *The Remove Background tool used to remove backgrounds from images.*

The Picture Tools Format Contextual Tab

The **Format** contextual tab of the **Picture Tools** tool tab provides commands that enable you to modify and enhance a picture. It contains the Adjust, Picture Styles, Arrange, and Size groups.

Group	*Allows You To*
Adjust	Fine-tune the color, brightness, and contrast of an object.
Picture Styles	Format the overall appearance of a picture including the shape, outline, border, and special effects.
Arrange	Position an object on a slide in relation to other objects or text.
Size	Resize, rotate, or crop an object.

Object Scaling

Scaling is the process of adjusting an object's height and width proportionately. You can select an option in the **Format Picture** dialog box to scale an object to suit specific requirements. The **Lock aspect ratio** option automatically adjusts the width when you change the height or vice versa to maintain the aspect ratio of the original object. The **Relative to original picture size** option scales a picture, based on the width and height of the original picture. The **Best scale for slide show** option adjusts a picture, based on the screen resolution that will be used to display the slide show.

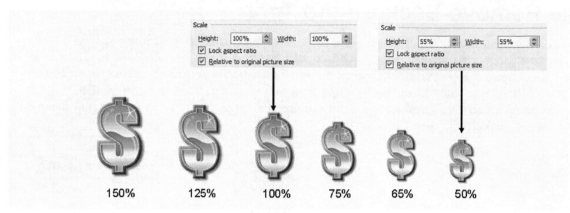

Figure 5-3: Scaling an object.

Graphical Object Orientation Options

Orientation, or rotation, is the angle at which an object appears on a slide. It is measured in degrees from 0 to 360. When you select an object, a rotation handle in the form of a circle appears along with the sizing handles. You can rotate the rotation handle clockwise or counter-clockwise to change the orientation of the object. Holding down **Shift** as you rotate the rotation handle causes the object to rotate in 15 degree increments.

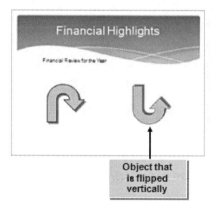

Figure 5-4: The selected object is flipped vertically.

You can also change the orientation of an object by using the options in the **Rotate** drop-down list in the **Arrange** group on the **Format** contextual tab.

Rotate Option	Used To
Rotate Right 90°	Rotate an object clockwise by 90°.
Rotate Left 90°	Rotate an object counterclockwise by 90°.
Flip Vertical	Reverse an object vertically.
Flip Horizontal	Reverse an object horizontally.
More Rotation Options	Rotate an object by a specific angle.

More Rotation Options

More rotation options allow you to rotate an object on a slide by a specific degree to create visually interesting effects on the slides. These options can be set in the **Size and rotate** section on the **Size** tab of **Format Picture** dialog box.

Image Compression Options

Image compression is a technique you can use to reduce the file size of an image. The more graphics you add to a PowerPoint presentation, the larger the file size becomes. Compressing the images significantly reduces the overall file size of your presentation. A presentation with a smaller file size makes sharing presentations using email or other electronic methods more manageable.

Selecting a Target Output

PowerPoint provides three target output options for compressing images.

Target Output Option	Description
Print (220 ppi)	Excellent quality on most printers and screens when saving the output for print.
Screen (150 ppi)	Good quality on web pages and projectors when saving the output for the web.
E-mail (96 ppi)	Image size is minimized when saving the output for sharing through email.

How to Edit Graphical Objects

Procedure Reference: Remove the Background of a Picture

To remove the background of a picture:

1. Select the picture from which you want to remove the background.
2. On the **Picture Tools Format** contextual tab, in the **Adjust** group, click **Remove Background** to display the **Background Removal** tab.
3. Adjust the shape and size of the marquee to cover the area of the picture you want to retain. The purple areas are those that will be removed.
4. If necessary, on the **Background Removal** tab, use the options in the **Refine** group to mark the areas to retain or remove.
    *   Click **Mark Areas to Keep** to draw lines to mark areas to keep in the picture.
    *   Click **Mark Areas to Remove** to draw lines to mark areas to remove in the picture.
    *   Click **Delete Mark** to delete lines you have drawn to change areas to keep or remove.
5. If necessary, in the **Refine** group, click **Discard All Changes** to exit the **Background Removal** tab and discard all changes.
6. View the result.
    *   On the **Background Removal** tab, in the **Refine** group, click **Keep Changes** to close the **Background Removal** tab and keep all changes or;
    *   Click outside the selection to view the edited picture.

Procedure Reference: Resize an Object

To resize an object:

1. Navigate to the slide that contains the object you want to format.
2. On the slide, select the object to display the sizing handles around it.
3. Resize the object.
   - Resize the object manually.
     - Drag a sizing handle toward the center of the object to reduce its size.
     - Drag a sizing handle away from the center of the object to enlarge it.
     - Hold down **Ctrl** and drag the sizing handle to keep the center of the object at the same place.
     - Hold down **Shift** and drag the sizing handle to maintain the original proportion of the object while resizing.
     - Hold down both **Ctrl** and **Shift** and drag the sizing handle to maintain both the original proportion and the center of the object.
   - Resize the object by using the commands on the **Format** contextual tab.
     a. On the Ribbon, select the **Format** contextual tab.
     b. In the **Size** group, resize the height and width of the object.
        - In the **Shape Height** text box, type a height for the object.
        - In the **Shape Width** text box, type a width for the object.

Selecting Objects Manually

PowerPoint 2010 provides the following techniques for selecting objects manually.

To Select	Do This
A single object	Click it.
More than one object	Hold down **Shift** and click the objects.
Multiple objects	Drag a selection marquee around the objects.
All of the objects	Press **Ctrl+A** to select them all.

Procedure Reference: Compress an Image

To compress an image:

1. Select the image that you want to compress.
2. On the **Format** contextual tab, in the **Adjust** group, click **Compress Pictures.**
3. In the **Compress Pictures** dialog box, check the **Apply only to this picture** check box.
4. If necessary, in the **Compress Pictures** dialog box, click **Options** to modify the compression settings.
   a. In the **Compression Settings** dialog box, in the **Compression Options** section, set options to compress the image.
      - Check the **Automatically Perform Basic Compression On Save** check box to save the compressed version of the image. This option applies only to the presentation that is open.

- Check the **Delete Cropped Areas Of Picture** check box to remove cropped areas from the picture.

b. In the **Target Output** section, set a target output.

5. Click **OK** to apply compression settings.

Procedure Reference: Change the Orientation of an Object

To change the orientation of an object:

1. Select the object that you want to rotate to view its sizing handles.

2. Rotate the object.
   - Rotate the object by using the rotation handles.
     - Drag the rotation handle in the required direction to display the object at an angle or;
     - Hold down **Shift** and drag the rotation handle in the required direction to rotate the object in 15 degree increments.
   - Rotate the object by using the options available in the **Rotate** drop-down list.
     a. On the Ribbon, select the **Format** contextual tab.
     b. In the **Arrange** group, from the **Rotate** drop-down list, select the desired rotation option.
   - Rotate the object by using the **Format Object** dialog box.
     a. On the **Picture Tools** tool tab, on the **Format** contextual tab, click the **Format Object** dialog box launcher.
     b. In the **Format Object** dialog box, in the **Size and rotate** section, in the **Rotation** text box, type a value.
     c. Click **Close** to apply the rotation to the object.

Procedure Reference: Scale an Object

To scale an object:

1. Select the object that you want to scale.

2. On the **Picture Tools** tool tab, on the **Format** contextual tab, in the **Size** group, click the **Size and Position** dialog box launcher.

3. In the **Format Picture** dialog box, in the **Scale** section, use the desired options to scale the object.
   - In the **Height** text box, specify the required height.
   - In the **Width** text box, specify the required width.
   - If necessary, check the **Lock Aspect Ratio** check box to scale the object proportionately.
   - If necessary, check the **Relative To Original Picture Size** check box to scale the object as a percentage of its original size.
   - If necessary, check the **Best Scale For Slide Show** check box and select a resolution.

4. Click **Close** to apply the scaling.

Procedure Reference: Crop a Picture

To crop a picture:

1. Select the object that you want to crop.

2. On the **Format** contextual tab, in the **Size** group, select the desired option.

● Click the **Crop** button and drag the sizing handles as desired or;

● Click the **Crop** drop-down arrow, and from the displayed gallery, select the desired shape or;

● From the **Aspect Ratio** drop-down list, select the desired aspect ratio.

ACTIVITY 5-1
Editing Images

Scenario:

While reviewing the slides you added to your presentation, you feel it would be more visually appealing and would establish relevance if the background of the image, in the About Us slide, is removed. You also want to compress the size of the picture to facilitate sharing the presentation through web or email. You realize that the clip art in the Revenue Details slide will look better if it was larger and positioned properly.

1. Remove the picture background.

    a. Navigate to the C:\084592Data\Modifying Graphical Objects in a Presentation folder and open the OGC Properties.pptx file.

    b. On the **Slides** tab, select slide 4 and on the slide, click the picture to select it.

    c. Select the **Format** contextual tab, and in the **Adjust** group, click **Remove Background.**

    d. Drag the left-middle handle of the background marquee to the left edge of the image.

    e. Similarly, drag the right-middle handle to the right edge of the image, and the bottom-center handle of the background marquee to the bottom edge of the image.

    f. On the **Background Removal** tab, in the **Refine** group, click **Mark Areas to Keep.**

    g. Click below the left ear of the man and then click slightly lower than the previous mark.

    h. On the **Background Removal** tab, in the **Close** group, click the **Keep Changes** button to remove the area shaded in pink from the image.

    i. Click outside the picture to deselect and observe that the background is removed from the image.

2. Compress the picture.

    a. Click the picture to select it.

    b. On the **Format** contextual tab, in the **Adjust** group, click the **Compress Pictures** button, which is the first button from the top.

    c.   In the **Compress Pictures** dialog box, verify that the **Apply only to this picture** check box is checked and click **OK.**

3.   Scale and position the clip art.

    a.   On the **Slides** tab, scroll down and select slide 10.

    b.   Select the clip art on the slide.

    c.   Select the **Format** contextual tab, and in the **Size** group, click the **Format Picture** dialog box launcher.

    d.   In the **Format Picture** dialog box, in the left pane, verify that the **Size** tab is selected.

    e.   In the right pane, in the **Size and rotate** section, in the **Height** text box, triple-click and type *2.9* and then press **Tab.**

    f.   Observe that the value in the **Width** text box has automatically changed to 2.89.

    g.   In the **Format Picture** dialog box, select the **Position** tab, and in the right pane, in the **Position on slide** section, in the **Horizontal** text box, triple-click and type *5.83*

    h.   In the **Vertical** text box, triple-click and type *3.08* and click **Close.**

    i.   Observe that the clip art is scaled as desired.

    j.   Save the file as *My OGC Properties* in the PPTX format.

ACTIVITY 5-2
Changing Object Orientation

Before You Begin:
The My OGC Properties.pptx file is open.

Scenario:
You have used arrow shapes to describe the flow of action on a slide in your presentation. You have received an update on the information that is to be presented. You want to include the updated information and highlight the same by making the necessary changes to the slide and by modifying the shapes and their orientation. Also, you want to enhance the visual appearance of the shapes to retain the audience's interest.

1. Rotate the shapes.

    a. On the **Slides** tab, select slide 8.

    b. Click the curved right arrow shape to select it.

    c. On the **Home** tab, in the **Clipboard** group, click the **Copy** button and then click the **Paste** button.

    d. Click and drag the newly created arrow to the right of the text boxes.

    e. On the **Drawing Tools** tool tab, select the **Format** contextual tab.

    f. In the **Arrange** group, from the **Rotate** drop-down list, select **Flip Vertical.**

    g. From the **Rotate** drop-down list, select **Flip Horizontal.**

2. Scale the shapes.

    a. On the **Format** contextual tab, in the **Size** group, click the **Format Picture** dialog box launcher.

    b. In the **Format Shape** dialog box, verify that the **Size** tab is selected.

    c. In the **Size and rotate** section, in the **Height** text box, triple-click and type *2.75* and click **Close.**

    d. Observe that the arrow has increased in size.

    e. Similarly, scale the other arrow.

    f. Move the arrows to align them to the text boxes. This will be done for you.

    g. Save the presentation.

TOPIC B
Format Graphical Objects

You edited graphical objects in a presentation. After manipulating the size and orientation of an object, you may sense that something is still missing—the object may be in the wrong color or may not have appropriate effects applied. In this topic, you will format the graphical objects on a slide.

At times, graphical objects may not complement the theme of a presentation or may not be appealing. But these objects might be integral to the message you are trying to convey. You can make minor alterations by formatting objects to significantly improve their appearance.

Object Formatting Options

The **Format Shape** dialog box provides various options that help format an object. The options that are available are determined by the type of object you are formatting.

Formatting Option	Allows You To
Fill	Change the fill color of an object.
Line	Change the color of a line or color of an object's border.
Line Style	Change the line styles of an object. It also allows you to add an arrow at the end of a line.
Shadow	Apply a shadow to an object.
3-D Format	Apply a three-dimensional effect to an object.
3-D Rotation	Change the orientation and perspective of an object with 3-D effect.
Text Box	Modify the text layout within a text box. This option is enabled only if the selected object is a shape or text box.
Picture Corrections	Adjust brightness, contrast, and sharpness of a picture.
Picture Color	Modify color saturation, color tone, and recolor a picture.

The Set Transparent Color Option

The **Set Transparent Color** option enables you to make one of the colors in a picture transparent. Selecting this option displays a small arrow at the edge of the mouse pointer, while clicking a color in a picture makes that color transparent.

Picture Formatting Options

The **Picture Styles** group on the **Format** contextual tab provides you with options to format pictures.

Option	Allows You To
Picture Border	Choose from various theme colors and the types and colors for the outline.
Picture Effects	Format a picture by using various picture effects. You can also use predefined picture effects.
Picture Layout	Select from various layouts for a picture.
Picture Styles	Apply overall visual style to a picture.

How to Format Graphical Objects

Procedure Reference: Format a Shape

To format a shape:

1. Select the object that you want to format.
2. Format the shape using the **Format** contextual tab.
    *   Format the shape by using the commands in the **Shape Styles** group.
        *   In the **Shape Styles** group, click the **More** button, and from the displayed gallery, select a shape style theme.
        *   From the **Shape Fill** drop-down list, select a color to change the fill color of the object.
        *   From the **Shape Outline** drop-down list, select the color, line style, and width of the line that marks the boundaries of the object.
        *   From the **Shape Effects** drop-down list, select a visual effect.
    *   Format the shape by using the **Format Shape** dialog box.
        a. In the **Shape Styles** group, click the **Format Shape** dialog box launcher.
        b. In the **Format Shape** dialog box, in the left pane, select a tab and in the right pane, specify the desired options to apply a format to the shape.
            *   Select the **Fill** tab, and in the right pane, select an option to fill the shape with color.
            *   Select the **Line Color** tab, and in the right pane, select an option for the line color.
            *   Select the **Line Style** tab, and in the right pane, select an option to choose a line style.
            *   Select the **Shadow** tab, and in the right pane, select a preset, and set the level of transparency, size, blur, angle, and distance.
            *   Select the **Reflection** tab, and in the right pane, select a preset and set the level of transparency, size, distance, and blur.
            *   Select the **Glow and Soft Edges** tab, and in the right pane, select a preset and a color and then set the level of size and transparency. In the **Soft Edges** section, select a preset and set the level of size.

- Select the **3-D Format** tab, and in the right pane, select a level, depth, and surface.
- Select the **3-D Rotation** tab, and in the right pane, select a rotation preset, and customize the rotation angles and object position.
- Select the **Position** tab, and in the right pane, set the level of horizontal and vertical positions on the slide and also set the location.
- Select the **Text Box** tab, and in the right pane, select the text layout, AutoFit, and internal margins.

Procedure Reference: Format a Picture

To format a picture:

1. Select the picture that you want to format.
2. Format the picture using the **Format** contextual tab.
   a. On the **Format** contextual tab, in the **Adjust** group, click the **Corrections** drop-down arrow.
   b. From the displayed gallery, in the **Sharpen and Soften** and **Brightness and Contrast** sections, select the desired options to correct the picture.
3. On the **Format** contextual tab, in the **Picture Styles** group, click the **Format Picture** dialog box launcher.
4. In the **Format Picture** dialog box set the options to format a picture.
   - In the **Sharpen and Soften** section, from the **Presets** section, select the desired option.
   - In the **Sharpen and Soften** section, move the slider to the desired level.
   - In the **Sharpen** spin box, set the desired value to sharpen the image.
   - In the **Brightness and Contrast** section, from the **Presets** section, select the desired options.
   - In the **Brightness and Contrast** section, move the slider to the desired level.
   - In the **Brightness** spin box, set the desired value to alter the brightness.
   - In the **Contrast** spin box, set the desired value to alter the contrast.
   - If necessary, click **Reset** to restore the picture to its original settings.

Procedure Reference: Set Transparent Color to an Object

To set transparent color to an object:

1. On the **Format** contextual tab, in the **Adjust** group, from the **Recolor** drop-down list, select **Set Transparent Color.**
2. Click a color in the image to make that color transparent.

Procedure Reference: Add Artistic Effects to an Image

To add artistic effects to an image:

1. Select the object to which you want to apply an artistic effect.
2. On the **Format** contextual tab, in the **Adjust** group, click the **Artistic Effects** drop-down arrow.
3. From the displayed gallery, select the desired artistic effect.

Procedure Reference: Change a Picture

To change a picture:

1. Select the picture you want to change.

2. On the **Format** contextual tab, in the **Adjust** group, click the **Change Picture** button to launch the **Insert Picture** dialog box.

3. In the **Insert Picture** dialog box, choose the desired picture and click **Insert.**

ACTIVITY 5-3
Formatting Objects on a Slide

Before You Begin:
The My OGC Properties.pptx file is open.

Scenario:
While reviewing your presentation, one of your colleagues suggests that the picture of Jane Doe used in the presentation should be brighter because the presentation will be delivered using an overhead projector. She also suggests that the text "OGC Properties" be made to look more visually appealing to give prominence to the first slide. Also, you want to make the background of the image in the Customer Expectations slide transparent to get the audience's focus on the main elements in the picture.

---

1. Apply a WordArt style and a shadow effect to the presentation title.

   a. In the left pane, scroll up and select slide 1.

   b. On the slide, triple-click the text "OGC Properties" to select it.

   c. Select the **Format** contextual tab, and in the **WordArt Styles** group, click the **More** button, and from the displayed gallery, in the **Applies to All Text in the Shape** section, select **Fill - Blue, Accent 2, Warm Matte Bevel,** which is the third WordArt in the first row.

   d. On the **Format** contextual tab, in the **WordArt Styles** group, click the **Text Effects** drop-down arrow, and in the drop-down list, hover the mouse pointer over **Shadow** to view the gallery.

   e. From the displayed gallery, in the **Outer** section, select **Offset Diagonal Top Left,** which is the third effect in the third row.

   f. Deselect the text to observe the effect applied to the text.

---

2. Change the brightness and contrast levels of the photograph of Jane Doe.

   a. In the left pane, scroll down and select slide 13.

   b. On the slide, click the photograph to select it.

   c. Select the **Format** contextual tab, and in the **Adjust** group, click the **Corrections** drop-down arrow and from the displayed gallery, in the **Brightness and Contrast** section, select the **Brightness: 0% (Normal) Contrast:-20%,** which is the third option in the second row.

---

3. Set the transparent color.

   a. In the left pane, scroll up, select slide 7, and on the slide, click the picture to select it.

   b. Select the **Format** contextual tab, and in the **Adjust** group, click the **Color** drop-down arrow and from the gallery, select **Set Transparent Color.**

   c. On the picture, click the gray color.

---

d.   Observe that the desired portion has become transparent.

e.   Click outside the picture to deselect it.

f.   Save the presentation.

TOPIC C
Group Graphical Objects on a Slide

You formatted a graphical object on a slide. Sometimes, a single slide may contain multiple objects for which you need to apply the same formatting. In this topic, you will group and ungroup graphical objects on a slide.

Slides may contain multiple objects that need to be repositioned or formatted alike. Positioning or formatting each object on a slide individually may take a lot of effort and might also result in errors. Rather than manually working on each object one at a time, PowerPoint provides you with options to work on the objects together, without disturbing their alignment or sequence. With this flexibility, you can manipulate multiple objects simultaneously, thus saving considerable time.

The Grouping Feature

Grouping is a technique by which multiple objects can be arranged together to form a single entity. Any modifications made to the group will then affect all of the objects in that group. When objects are grouped, there will be one single set of sizing handles for the entire group; therefore, the entire group can be moved or resized as a whole. However, PowerPoint also allows you to modify individual objects within a group by first selecting the group and then selecting an object within the group that you want to modify.

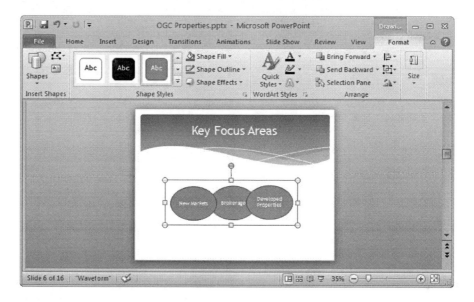

Figure 5-5: *A slide displaying grouped objects.*

You can also separate grouped objects using a technique called *ungrouping*. When a group is ungrouped, individual objects will then have their own sizing handles and can be modified independently.

How to Group Graphical Objects on a Slide

Procedure Reference: Group Objects

To group objects:

1. Select the objects on the slide that you want to group.

2. Group the selected objects.

   - On the **Format** contextual tab, in the **Arrange** group, from the **Group** drop-down list, select **Group** or;

   - Right-click the selected objects, and from the shortcut menu, choose **Group→Group.**

3. If necessary, resize, modify, or move the grouped objects.

   - Resize the grouped objects by dragging the sizing handles to the desired size.

   - Modify the grouped objects to the shape and color you want by using the **Shape Styles** group on the **Format** contextual tab.

   - On the **Format** contextual tab, in the **Size** group, display the **Format Shape** dialog box launcher and select the desired option.

     ■ On the **Position** tab, in the **Position On Slide** section, in the **Horizontal** and **Vertical** text boxes, type the position of the grouped objects.

     ■ On the **Size** tab, in the **Size** section, set the desired settings.

   - In the **Size** group, click the **Format Shape** dialog box launcher and select the desired option.

     a. Click **Close** to close the **Format Shape** dialog box.

Procedure Reference: Ungroup Objects

To ungroup objects:

1. On the slide, select the grouped objects that you want to ungroup.

2. Ungroup the objects.

   - On the **Format** contextual tab, in the **Arrange** group, from the **Group** drop-down list, select **Ungroup** or;

   - Right-click the selected objects, and from the shortcut menu, choose **Group→Ungroup.**

ACTIVITY 5-4
Grouping and Ungrouping Objects on a Slide

Before You Begin:
The My OGC Properties.pptx file is open.

Scenario:
You have multiple objects on a slide for which you want to apply effects. Applying effects to objects individually will be time consuming. Also, you want to make sure that the effect you apply is uniform across all the objects.

---

1. Align the objects on the Key Focus Areas slide.

    a. In the left pane, scroll down and select slide 11.

    b. Select the first blue oval shape, which contains the text "New Markets," hold down **Shift,** and select the remaining shapes.

    c. Select the **Format** contextual tab, and in the **Arrange** group, from the **Group** drop-down list, select **Group** to group the selected objects.

    d. Observe that only one resizing handle is displayed for the grouped objects.

    e. In the **Arrange** group, from the **Align** drop-down list, select **Align Center** to position the group in the horizontal center.

    f. From the **Align** drop-down list, select **Align Middle** to position the group in the vertical center.

---

2. Ungroup the objects.

    a. On the **Format** contextual tab, in the **Arrange** group, from the **Group** drop-down list, select **Ungroup.**

    b. Observe that the objects are ungrouped and have independent sizing handles.

    c. Click outside the shapes to deselect them.

    d. Save the presentation.

TOPIC D
Arrange Graphical Objects on a Slide

You grouped objects on a slide. When displaying multiple objects on a slide, you may need to show the critical objects in front of the other objects on the slide. In this topic, you will arrange graphical objects on a slide.

For complex slides that have a number of objects, if the arrangement is not properly done, it may appear chaotic. For this reason, you need to layer the objects on a slide in a specific order. Furthermore, you might need to align objects that are unevenly placed. By arranging the objects on a slide in an appropriate order, you can create more complex graphics and enhance comprehension. Rather than settling for solitary images, you can build layer images and carefully determine their position on the screen to give you a great deal of flexibility and control.

Order of Objects

The *order of objects* determines how overlapping objects appear in relation to each other on a slide. The object in the front layer will be completely visible, whereas the visibility of the object in the back layer may be obstructed by the objects in front of it. You can also change the order of objects to display only the required areas of the overlapped image.

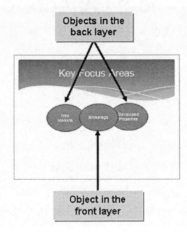

Figure 5-6: Overlapping objects on a slide.

The **Arrange Objects** group on the **Format** contextual tab contains options that you can use to order objects.

Option	Description
Bring Forward	Places an object at the front of another object that is in front of it.
Bring To Front	Brings an object in front of all the objects.
Send Backward	Places an object at the back of the object that is behind it.
Send To Back	Places an object at the back of all the objects.

Guides and Gridlines

Guides are lines that enable you to position objects on a slide. By default, PowerPoint provides you with a vertical and a horizontal guide that divide a slide into four equal quadrants. You can move or add additional guides as necessary. *Gridlines* are multiple dotted lines that appear horizontally and vertically on a slide. Gridlines further divide a slide into much smaller squares of equal dimensions. You cannot move gridlines, but can adjust the width between them. Gridlines provide visual cues to enable you to arrange and align objects on a slide. You can even set the objects to snap to grid to align them.

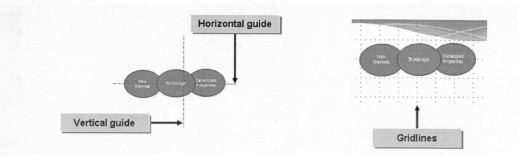

Figure 5-7: Gridlines and guides on a slide.

How to Arrange Graphical Objects on a Slide

Procedure Reference: Arrange Objects

To arrange objects:

1. Navigate to the slide that contains objects that you want to arrange in order.
2. Select the object for which you need to set the order.
3. On the **Format** contextual tab, in the **Arrange** group, select an ordering option.
    *   Click **Bring Forward** to bring the object one step closer to the front.
    *   Click **Send Backward** to send the object one step back.
    *   Click **Bring to Front** to bring the object in front of all the objects.
    *   Click **Send to Back** to place the object behind all the objects.
4. If necessary, arrange other objects on the slide.

Procedure Reference: Align Objects by Using Guides

To align objects by using guides:

1. Select the objects that you want to align.
2. On the **Format** contextual tab, in the **Arrange** group, from the **Align** drop-down list, select **Grid Settings.**
3. In the **Grid and Guides** dialog box, in the **Guide Settings** section, check the **Display Drawing Guides On Screen** check box and click **OK.**
4. If necessary, hold down **Ctrl** and drag the existing guides to add additional guides.
5. Using the guides as a reference, drag the selected objects to position them on the slide.

Procedure Reference: Align Objects by Using Gridlines

To align objects by using gridlines:

1. Select the objects that you want to align.

2.   Display the gridlines.

*   On the **View** tab, in the **Show** group, check the **Gridlines** check box or;

*   On the **Format** contextual tab, in the **Arrange** group, from the **Align** drop-down list, select **Show Gridlines** or;

*   Display the gridlines by using the **Grid and Guides** dialog box.

   a.   On the **Format** contextual tab, in the **Arrange** group, from the **Align** drop-down list, select **Grid Settings.**

   b.   In the **Grid and Guides** dialog box, in the **Grid Settings** section, check the **Display Grid On Screen** check box.

   c.   If necessary, in the **Grid and Guides** dialog box, in the **Grid Settings** section, in the **Spacing** text box, type the spacing you want for the grids.

   d.   Click **OK** to close the **Grid and Guides** dialog box.

3.   Using the grids as a reference, align the objects precisely, particularly in relation to each other.

ACTIVITY 5-5
Arranging the Order of Objects on a Slide

Before You Begin:

The My OGC Properties.pptx file is open.

Scenario:

You are making minor aesthetic changes to the OGC Properties presentation before delivering it. On a particular slide, you want to give a neat and professional look by arranging the objects that are overlapping. You want to use grids and guides to ensure that you place the objects in their apt positions.

1. Arrange the shapes that contain text.

    a. Click the shape containing the text "New Markets" to select it.

    b. Select the **Format** contextual tab, and in the **Arrange** group, from the **Send Backward** drop-down list, select **Send to Back.**

    c. Observe that the shape is moved behind the shape containing the text "Brokerage."

    d. Click the shape containing the text "Brokerage" to select it.

    e. On the **Format** contextual tab, in the **Arrange** group, from the **Bring Forward** drop-down list, select **Bring to Front.**

    f. Click outside the shape to deselect it.

2. Reposition the objects on the slide.

    a. In the left pane, select slide 12.

    b. Select the **View** tab, and in the **Show** group, check the **Guides** check box.

c. Click the horizontal guide and drag it to 0.25 inch above zero of the vertical ruler so that it aligns with the top border of the shapes containing the text "Quality Control" and "Project Evaluation."

d. Select all the objects on the slide. This will be done for you.

e. Select the **Format** contextual tab, in the **Arrange** group, from the **Align** drop-down list, select **Align Middle.**

f. In the **Arrange** group, from the **Align** drop-down list, select **Distribute Horizontally.**

g. Select the **View** tab and uncheck the **Guides** check box.

h. Deselect the objects on the slide.

i. Save the presentation.

TOPIC E
Apply Animation Effects

You arranged objects on a slide. Presentations that contain a lot of static content, such as text or graphics, can become monotonous for the audience. In this topic, you will apply animation effects in a presentation.

When you present slides that contain just static objects and text, you run the risk of losing the attention of the audience. Animating the objects on a slide and adding special effects will help you keep the audience engaged.

The Built-in Animation Effects

Built-in animations in PowerPoint are readily available animation effects that apply movement and dynamic effects to an object or text on a slide during a slide show. You can apply animation to a single object or to multiple objects on a slide. PowerPoint provides various built-in animations that you can use to make your presentation more captivating.

Built-in animation effects allow you to control the visual prominence of a slide object.

Animation Effect	Description
Fade	Objects become visible slowly on the slide.
Wipe	Objects appear by rolling up from the bottom of the slide to the top.
Grow & Turn	Objects appear by turning and increasing in size.
Bounce	Objects appear by bouncing.
Fly In	Objects fly in on a slide.

The Animation Painter Feature

The *Animation Painter* feature provides you with an easy way to animate objects. You can use this feature to copy the animation applied to an existing object on a slide and apply it to other objects. When you double-click the **Animation Painter** button, you will be in a Sticky Mode, which helps you apply a desired animation effect to multiple objects not only in the same presentation, but also in different presentations.

How to Apply Animation Effects

Procedure Reference: Apply Built-in Animations to an Object or Text

To apply built-in animations to an object or text on a slide:

1. Select the object or text on a slide to which you want to apply an animation.
2. On the **Animations** tab, in the **Animations** group, click the **More** drop-down arrow, and from the displayed gallery, select an animation.
3. If necessary, preview the presentation to view the animation that you set.

Procedure Reference: Remove Built-in Animations from an Object or Text

To remove built-in animations from an object or text:

1. Select the object for which you want to remove the animation.
2. On the **Animations** tab, in the **Animations** group, from the **More** drop-down list, select **None.**
3. If necessary, preview the presentation to verify that the animation is removed.

Procedure Reference: Animate Objects by Using the Animation Painter Feature

To animate objects by using the Animation Painter feature:

1. Select the object that has the animation effect you want to copy.
2. On the **Animations** tab, in the **Advanced Animation** group, double-click the **Animation Painter** button to copy the existing object's animation.
3. Click the object to which you want to apply the copied animation effect.
4. If necessary, apply the same animation to multiple objects within the presentation by double-clicking the **Animation Painter** button and clicking on the desired objects.
5. Click outside the slide to deactivate the **Animation Painter** button.

ACTIVITY 5-6
Applying Animation Effects

Before You Begin:
The My OGC Properties.pptx file is open.

Scenario:
Your manager asks you to incorporate some special effects that help animate text and keep the audience's attention in track. He suggests that you animate the title slide to draw the audience's attention, while starting a presentation.

1. Apply the **Fade** animation to the title placeholder.

    a. In the left pane, scroll up and select slide 1.

    b. Select the title text placeholder containing the text "OGC Properties."

    c. Select the **Animations** tab, and in the **Animation** group, select **Fade.**

2. Apply the **Wipe** animation to the subtitle placeholder.

    a. Click the text box containing the text "Making your real estate dreams a reality" to select the text box.

    b. On the **Animations** tab, in the **Animation** group, click the **More** button, and from the displayed gallery, in the **Entrance** section, select **Wipe.**

3. Apply the **Fly In** animation to the text box containing version information.

    a. Click in the text box containing the version information.

    b. On the **Animations** tab, in the **Animation** group, select **Fly In.**

4. Run the slide show and check whether the animations are applied correctly.

    a. Select the **Slide Show** tab, and in the **Start Slide Show** group, click **From Beginning.**

    b. Click the slide to proceed.

    c. Observe that the title text is animated and then click the slide to proceed.

    d. Observe that the animation is applied to the text box containing the text "Making your real estate dreams a reality" and click the slide to proceed.

    e. Observe that the animation is applied to the text box containing the version information.

    f. Right-click anywhere on the slide and from the context menu, choose **End Show.**

    g. Save and close the presentation.

Lesson 5 Follow-up

In this lesson, you modified graphical objects. You can maintain the focus of an audience on just the most relevant aspects of the presentation by customizing the graphical objects to meet the specific needs of your presentation.

1. **What formatting techniques will you use the most often on the objects in your presentation?**

2. **What are the advantages of grouping and ordering graphical objects in your presentations?**

6 Working with Tables

Lesson Time: 30 minutes

Lesson Objectives:

In this lesson, you will work with tables in a presentation.

You will:

● Insert a table in a slide.

● Format tables.

● Import tables from other Microsoft Office applications.

Introduction

You modified various objects in a presentation. Presenting complex data in a simplified format is necessary for better understanding. In this lesson, you will work with tables for presenting complex data.

If complex information is presented as mere text, your audience may find it difficult to comprehend its importance or relevance. By using tables, you can display the information in such a manner that your audience can quickly grasp its meaning, particularly when comparing values.

TOPIC A
Insert a Table

You applied animation effects to objects on a PowerPoint slide. A large part of the presentation will be made up of text and supporting graphical objects. But, you also have to communicate complex data. In this topic, you will insert table in a slide.

Some information such as financial data needs to be presented in a structured manner, without which the information would lose its clarity. Presenting such data in the form of a bulleted list or paragraph often affects clarity, and the audience might not understand what you are trying to convey. Using a table to present such data can help you effectively bring out the relationships among data.

Tables

Definition:

A *table* is a grid-style container used for organizing data. It consists of boxes called *cells,* which can be arranged both vertically and horizontally to create *columns* and *rows,* respectively. There are various *border* styles that can be applied to a table. Tables can be small, simple, and conventional, or they can be quite extensive and complicated, even containing pictures.

Example:

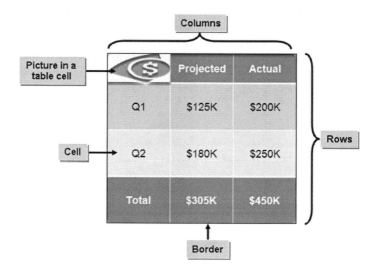

Figure 6-1: *A table with data.*

Table Creation Options

PowerPoint 2010 enables you to create tables dynamically by simply moving the mouse pointer over the checkered table displayed in the **Tables** group and selecting the number of rows and columns required. You can see a live preview of the table on the slide. You can create a table using the **Insert Table** option or manually draw a table using the **Draw Table** button.

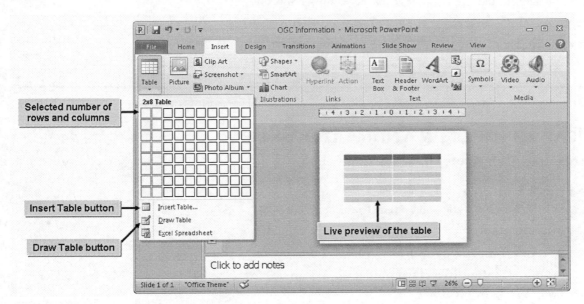

Figure 6-2: A dynamically created table.

The Insert Table Dialog Box

The **Insert Table** dialog box allows you to insert a table into a PowerPoint presentation. It contains spin boxes to specify the number of columns and rows for a table. After creating a table by using this dialog box, you can enter data in the rows and columns.

Figure 6-3: Options to specify the number of rows and columns in the Insert Table dialog box.

Add New Rows to a Table

You can place the insertion point in the cell, in the last row and last column of a table, and press **Tab** to quickly insert a new row at the bottom of the table.

Table Navigation Methods

PowerPoint provides you with several methods for navigating within a table using a keyboard.

Navigation Option	*Press*
Move one cell to the right	**Tab** or the **Right Arrow** key.
Move one cell to the left	**Shift+Tab** or the **Left Arrow** key.
Move down one row	The **Down Arrow** key.
Move up one row	The **Up Arrow** key.

How to Insert a Table in a Slide

Procedure Reference: Insert a Table

To insert a table:

1. On the Ribbon, select the **Insert** tab.

2. Insert the table.

    -   Insert a table by using the **Insert Table** option.

        a. On the **Insert** tab, in the **Tables** group, from the **Table** drop-down list, select **Insert Table.**

        b. In the **Insert Table** dialog box, enter the number of rows and columns that you want in the table.

        c. Click **OK** to insert the table.

    -   Insert a table by using grids.

        a. On the **Insert** tab, in the **Tables** group, in the **Table** drop-down list, place the mouse pointer over the cells in the grid to select the number of rows and columns you want in the table. Each cell in the grid represents one cell in the table.

        b. Click to insert the table.

    -   Insert a table by using the **Draw Table** option.

        a. On the **Insert** tab, in the **Tables** group, from the **Table** drop-down list, select **Draw Table.**

        b. Using the **Pen** tool, draw the table on the slide with the number of rows and columns you want in the table.

3. If necessary, position the table on the slide.

4. If necessary, resize the table.

Procedure Reference: Enter Data in a Table

To enter data in a table:

1. Place the insertion point in the appropriate cell in the table.

2. Type the information.

3. Navigate to the next cell and enter the desired information.

ACTIVITY 6-1
Inserting a Table

Data Files:

C:\084592Data\Working with Tables\OGC Properties.pptx

Scenario:

You have received the latest revenue details of the company and need to include them in the presentation that you are working on. To do this, you need to create a table to display the information.

Quarter	Projected	Actual
Q1	$125K	$200K
Q2	$180K	$250K
Total	$305K	$450K

1. Insert a table with four rows and three columns.

   a. Navigate to the C:\084592Data\Working with Tables folder and open the OGC Properties.pptx file.

   b. Select the **View** tab, and in the **Show** group, uncheck the **Ruler** check box.

   c. On the **Slides** tab, select slide 10.

   d. Select the **Insert** tab, and in the **Tables** group, click the **Table** drop-down arrow. From the displayed gallery, in the **Insert Table** section, select the cell in the third column in the fourth row.

   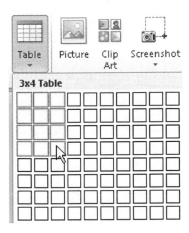

   e. Observe that a new table with four rows and three columns is inserted in the slide.

2. Enter the data in the table.

    a.   In the first row, in the first cell, click and type ***Quarter*** and press **Tab.**

    b.   Type ***Projected*** and press **Tab.**

    c.   Type ***Actual*** and press **Tab.**

    d.   Similarly, enter data in the last two rows as shown in the table in the scenario.

TOPIC B
Format Tables

You inserted a table in a slide. Tables often contain a great deal of information that the audience must comprehend in a short span of time. So, it becomes necessary to improve the readability and appearance of the table. In this topic, you will format tables.

Tables display a wealth of information. By modifying the format of a table, you can display information more clearly to the audience. Instead of relying on only textual content, you can also insert images into a table, or change the appearance of the table to blend with the overall design of the presentation.

The Design Contextual Tab

The commands on the **Design** contextual tab enable you to apply various table styles, add visual effects, and customize borders.

Command Group	Allows You To
Table Style Options	Format rows and columns in a table.
Table Styles	Apply various table styles to a table.
WordArt Styles	Add visual effects to the text in a table.
Draw Borders	Customize the borders of a table.

Table Style Options

You can modify the formatting style of tables by checking or unchecking the relevant check boxes in the **Table Style Options** group.

Check Box	Allows You To
Header Row	Modify the formatting style of a table header row.
First Column	Modify the formatting style of the first column.
Last Column	Modify the formatting style of the last column.
Total Row	Show or hide totals, which are displayed at the bottom of a table.
Banded Rows	Display or hide formatting for alternate rows.
Banded Columns	Display or hide formatting for alternate columns.

The Table Styles Feature

Table styles are a combination of formatting options, including color settings that can be applied to a table. When a table is inserted, a table style is applied to it by default. However, you can change the look of a table by selecting from the various options displayed in the **Table Styles** gallery.

The Table Effects Feature

Effects are a set of options that you can use to apply to a table. PowerPoint provides you with three table effect options to modify and enhance tables or individual cells within them.

Table Effect	Description
Cell Bevel	Adds a bevel effect to individual cells or an entire table.
Shadow	Adds a shadow effect to a table.
Reflection	Adds a mirror reflection effect to a table.

The Layout Contextual Tab

The **Layout** contextual tab includes groups of commands for modifying the layout of a table on a slide.

Group	Allows You To
Table	Select rows or columns of a table, display gridlines, or delete rows, columns, and cells of a table.
Rows & Columns	Insert rows or columns in a table.
Merge	Merge cells.
Cell Size	Set the row height or the column width of a table.
Alignment	Change the orientation of text and specify the margins of a selected cell.
Table Size	Set the height and width of a table.
Arrange	Arrange selected objects and display the selection pane.

The Alignment Group

The **Alignment** group on the **Layout** contextual tab contains various options for aligning text in a cell.

Option	Allows You To
Align Text Left	Align text to the left of a cell.
Center	Align text to the center of a cell.
Align Text Right	Align text to the right of a cell.
Align Top	Position text on top of a cell.
Center Vertically	Position text in the vertical center of a cell.
Align Bottom	Position text at the bottom of a cell.
Text Direction	Determine the direction in which text will be displayed in a cell.
Cell Margins	Specify the margins for the selected cells.

The Text Direction Drop-Down List

The **Text Direction** drop-down list contains various options to change the orientation of the text in a table. PowerPoint provides options such as **Horizontal, Rotate all Text 90°, Rotate all Text 270°,** and **Stacked.** These options are language specific.

Table Fill Options

The **Fill** tab in the **Format Shape** dialog box includes various options to fill a table cell with a color, picture, or texture.

Option	Description
No fill	Removes the fill from a cell.
Solid fill	Fills a cell with a solid color.
Gradient fill	Fills a table cell with a gradient of colors.
Picture or texture fill	Inserts a picture in a table cell.
Pattern fill	Fills a table cell with a pattern.

How to Format Tables

Procedure Reference: Format Tables by Using Contextual Tabs

To format tables by using contextual tabs:

1. Select the table that you want to format.
2. On the **Table Tools** tab, select the **Design** contextual tab.
3. In the **Table Style Options** group, check the desired check box to modify the formatting style.
4. In the **Table Styles** group, select the various options to apply the table styles and effects.
   - In the **Table Styles** gallery, select a table style option.
   - From the **Shading** drop-down list, select a background color option.
   - From the **Borders** drop-down list, select a border style option.
   - From the **Effects** drop-down list, select a table effect option.
5. On the **Table Tools** tab, select the **Layout** contextual tab.
6. If necessary, select a row or column to edit it.
   - Place the mouse pointer at the edge of the row you want to select and click to select the entire row or;
   - Place the mouse pointer at the edge of the column you want to select and click to select the entire column or;
   - On the **Layout** contextual tab, in the **Table** group, from the **Select** drop-down list, select **Select Column** or **Select Row** to select a column or row.
7. If necessary, in the **Merge** group, select an option to merge or split cells.
   - Click the **Merge Cells** button to merge cells.
   - Click the **Split Cells** button to split cells.

8. If necessary, in the **Cell Size** group, set a sizing option.

- In the **Height** text box, specify a value to set the height of the selected cells.
- In the **Width** text box, specify a value to set the width of the selected cells.
- Click the **Distribute Rows** button to distribute the height of the selected rows.
- Click the **Distribute Columns** button to distribute the width of the selected columns.

9. If necessary, in the **Alignment** group, set an alignment option.

10. If necessary, in the **Alignment** group, from the **Text Direction** drop-down list, select an option to change the orientation of the text.

11. If necessary, in the **Arrange** group, select an option to set the position of the table on the slide.

Procedure Reference: Add an Image to a Table

To add an image to a table:

1. Click the cell in which you want to insert an image.

2. Open the **Format Shape** dialog box.

- On the **Home** tab, in the **Drawing** group, click the **Format Shape** dialog box launcher or;
- Right-click the cell and choose **Format Shape.**

3. In the **Format Shape** dialog box, select **Fill.**

4. In the **Fill** section, select **Picture or texture fill.**

5. Insert an image into the cell.

- Insert clip art.

   a. In the **Insert from** section, click **Clip Art.**

   b. In the **Select Picture** dialog box, in the **Search text** text box, type a search word that best describes the clip art you want.

   c. Click **Go.**

   d. From the displayed results, select the clip art that you want to insert and click **OK.**

- Insert a picture from a file.

   a. In the **Insert from** section, click **File.**

   b. In the **Insert Picture** dialog box, navigate to the folder that contains the picture and select the picture.

   c. Click **Insert.**

6. In the **Format Shape** dialog box, click **Close.**

7. If necessary, drag the image to position it within the cell.

ACTIVITY 6-2
Formatting a Table

Before You Begin:
The My OGC Properties.pptx file is open.

Scenario:
You have created a table and want to make sure that the table colors suit your presentation requirements. Also, you want to ensure that the table is properly aligned and the information highlighted.

1. Modify the table style.

   a. Click the border of the table to select the entire table.

   b. Verify that the displayed table is selected, and on the **Design** contextual tab, in the **Table Style Options** group, check the **Total Row** check box.

2. Apply a table effect.

   a. In the **Table Styles** group, from the **Effects** drop-down list, select **Shadow.**

   b. From the displayed gallery, in the **Inner** section, select the **Inside Top** effect, which is the second effect in the first row.

3. Align the data in the cells.

   a. Select the **Layout** contextual tab, and in the **Alignment** group, click the **Center** button.

   b. On the **Layout** contextual tab, in the **Table Size** group, in the **Height** text box, click and type *2.0* and press **Enter.**

   c. In the **Width** text box, click and type *4.2* and press **Enter.**

   d. In the **Alignment** group, click **Center Vertically,** which is placed second from the left in the second row.

   e. Click and drag the table to the right corner of the slide.

   f. Save the presentation.

TOPIC C

Import Tables from Other Microsoft Office Applications

You formatted a table in a PowerPoint presentation. However, you may want to use a table from other applications such as Microsoft Excel or Microsoft Word. In this topic, you will import tables from other Office applications.

For a presentation, you may need to use data from tables in Microsoft Word or Excel files. Creating a new table and manually transferring the information will take a lot of effort and also create opportunities for error. PowerPoint provides you with the option to import tables from other applications, thereby saving you time and effort and at the same time ensuring that the data is accurate.

Linking vs. Embedding

You can use an external object such as a chart, graphic, table, or sound file in a presentation by either *linking* or *embedding* it on a slide. When an object is linked, data is physically stored in the source file, which is the original file containing the object. The object in the destination file merely acts as a window to view this data. When you modify the data in the source file, the object in the destination file automatically reflects the changes. When an object is embedded, there is no link between the data in the source and destination files. A copy of the data is physically embedded in the destination file and does not change if you modify the source file.

The Insert Object Dialog Box

The **Insert Object** dialog box allows you to insert an external object into a PowerPoint presentation. You can either create a file as an object or browse for objects stored on your computer to insert them into a presentation. You can also choose to display objects as icons in a presentation.

How to Import Tables from Other Microsoft Office Applications

Procedure Reference: Insert a Table from Other Applications

To insert a table from other applications:

1. Select the slide in which you want to insert a table.

2. On the **Insert** tab, in the **Text** group, click **Object.**

3. In the **Insert Object** dialog box, select **Create from file** to insert a table from another application.

4. In the **Insert Object** dialog box, click **Browse.**

5. In the **Browse** dialog box, navigate to the folder that contains the table, select the table, and click **OK.**

6. In the **Insert Object** dialog box, click **OK** to insert the table in the presentation.

Procedure Reference: Insert a Microsoft Excel Spreadsheet

To insert a Microsoft Excel spreadsheet:

1. Select the desired columns and rows in an Excel spreadsheet and copy them into the clipboard.

2. Switch to the PowerPoint application and select the desired slide.

3. On the slide, paste the copied content.

4. If necessary, resize the table as desired.

ACTIVITY 6-3
Inserting a Table from a Word Document

Data Files:

C:\084592Data\Working with Tables\Highlights Table.docx

Before You Begin:

The My OGC Properties.pptx file is open.

Scenario:

You want to include information in a slide on the financial highlights of your organization. Your colleague has provided you with necessary data in the form of a Word document. You want to insert this information into your presentation without having to manually enter it.

1. Insert a table from the Microsoft Word document.

    a. In the left pane, on the **Slides** tab, select slide 11.

    b. Select the **Insert** tab, and in the **Text** group, click **Object.**

    c. In the **Insert Object** dialog box, select the **Create from file** option and click **Browse.**

    d. In the **Browse** dialog box, navigate to the C:\084592Data\Working with Tables folder.

    e. Select the **Highlights Table.docx** file and click **OK.**

    f. In the **Insert Object** dialog box, click **OK** to insert the table.

2. Align the inserted data.

    a. On the **Format** contextual tab, in the **Arrange** group, from the **Align** drop-down list, select **Align Center.**

    b. Save the presentation.

    c. Close the presentation.

Lesson 6 Follow-up

In this lesson, you added tables to a presentation. Tables enable you to present complex information to your audience in an organized manner to enable easier comprehension.

1. **How does using tables to display text or data make your presentations more effective?**

2. **What formatting changes might you make to a table after adding it to a presentation?**

7 Working with Charts

Lesson Time: 30 minutes

Lesson Objectives:

In this lesson, you will add charts to a presentation.

You will:

- Insert charts.
- Modify a chart.
- Import charts from other Microsoft Office applications.

Introduction

You inserted tables in slides for presenting data. Sometimes, a graphical representation of data will facilitate better analysis by enabling you to relate to and compare data. In this lesson, you will add charts to a presentation.

Information presented as complex numerical data needs graphical representation, otherwise the presentation becomes less engaging. Adding charts to a presentation helps you create a visual relationship of numerical information. Charts also enhance text on slides and help you make a definitive statement.

TOPIC A

Insert Charts

You have presented statistical data in your presentation by using tables. Analyzing and comparing complex data becomes easier when it is presented as charts. In this topic, you will insert a chart in a presentation.

If your presentation contains extensive numeric information, the audience might find it difficult to analyze data. Analyzing and comparing numerical data requires more effort to comprehend when compared to the information presented visually. By presenting numerical data visually, you can establish the relationship between different sets of data for the audience to easily analyze.

Charts

Definition:

A *chart* is a visual representation of data. It can represent numeric data, quantitative structures, and functions. Charts show the relationship between groups of numerical data and may contain a *title, legend, data label,* and data table.

Example:

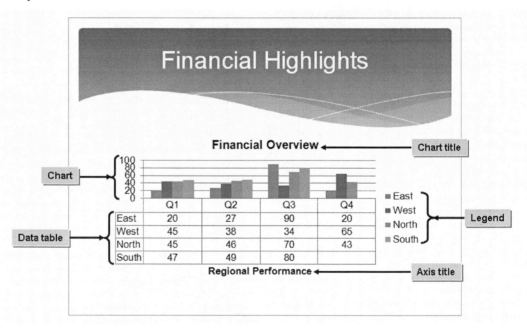

Figure 7-1: *A chart displaying data.*

The Chart Pane

The *Chart pane* is displayed by default when you insert a chart in a slide. It contains a sample chart plotted based on the data in an Excel worksheet. The **Chart** pane provides a preview of how the chart will look after you finalize the settings and enter the data.

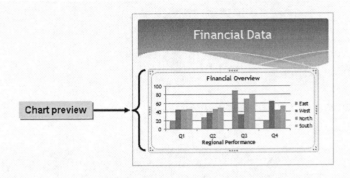

Figure 7-2: The Chart pane containing a chart.

Chart Data

When you insert a chart in a slide, the sample data used for creating the chart is displayed in an Excel worksheet. The sample data contains row and column headings, which are used in the chart as data labels. You can add, remove, or change the data in the worksheet according to your needs. The Excel worksheet is saved along with the PowerPoint file.

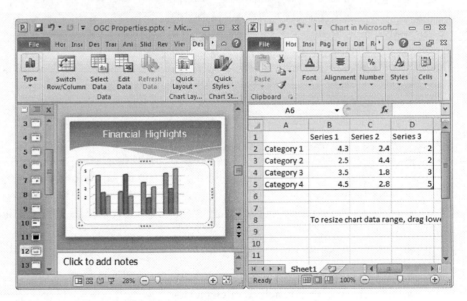

Figure 7-3: An Excel worksheet containing sample data.

The Switch Rows/Columns Feature

The *Switch rows/columns* feature enables you to swap data between the axes, without having to enter the data again. The data charted on the X-axis will become the Y-axis data, and vice versa.

Chart Tools

The contextual **Chart Tools** tool tab includes commands that enable you to modify and enhance the design and layout of charts in PowerPoint. The chart formatting commands are distributed on the **Design, Layout,** and **Format** contextual tabs.

Figure 7-4: Chart tools on the Design contextual tab.

Figure 7-5: Chart tools on the Layout contextual tab.

Figure 7-6: Chart tools on the Format contextual tab.

Contextual Tab	Allows You To
Design	<ul><li>Change the chart type and save the formatting and layout of a chart as a template for future charts.</li><li>Switch between rows and columns. It also allows you to select, edit, and refresh data.</li><li>Change the overall layout of a chart and the overall visual style of a chart.</li></ul>
Layout	<ul><li>Format chart elements, insert pictures, shapes, and text boxes.</li><li>Add, remove, or position chart elements.</li><li>Change the formatting of the axis and switch on and off gridlines.</li><li>Format chart background elements such as Plot Area, Chart Wall, Chart Floor, and 3-D Rotation.</li><li>Analyze Trendline, Lines, Up/down Bars, and Error Bars.</li></ul>
Format	<ul><li>Choose a visual style for a shape, line, or text.</li><li>Arrange, align, group, and rotate the elements on a chart.</li><li>Change the size and position of an object on a chart.</li></ul>

The Save As Template Feature

The *Save As Template* feature enables you to save and reuse a chart type as a chart template. This feature enables you to easily create new charts based on the template, instead of customizing each chart after you create it.

Chart Types

PowerPoint includes various chart types that you can use in your presentations. Each chart type has a list of subtypes for displaying data in various ways and highlighting different aspects.

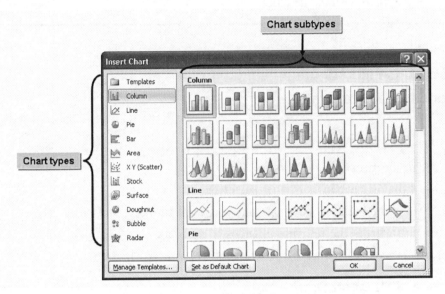

Figure 7-7: Chart types available in PowerPoint.

Chart Type	Description
Column	A chart type that compares data in a column format.
Line	A chart type that plots the change in data over a period of time, and is represented as one or more linear lines.
Pie	A chart type that displays data as a proportion (or percentage) of a whole, and is displayed as wedges of a pie. The greater the proportion, the larger the wedge.
Bar	A chart type that displays the frequencies or comparative value of data, as represented by the length of each bar.
Area	Similar to a line chart, an area chart emphasizes the magnitude of change over time, showing the cumulative value across a trend. Data is often stacked and represented with differing colors.
XY(Scatter)	A chart type that takes the numerical data points from the x-axis, and the data points from the y-axis and combines the data points from each set into one single set of data points. The data points of this chart type are often displayed in uneven intervals or clusters.

Chart Type	Description
Stock	A chart type that plots data in a stock chart. This type of chart illustrates the fluctuation of stock prices.
Doughnut	A chart type that is similar to a pie chart. This chart type displays the relationship of parts to a whole of more than one data series.
Bubble	A chart type that displays multi-dimensional data in the format of a bubble, in which the bubble size corresponds to the data values.
Radar	A chart type that compares the aggregate values of several data series that are plotted along multiple axes. For example, a radar chart can be used to track temperature over a given period of time for multiple cities.

How to Insert Charts

Procedure Reference: Create a Chart

To create a chart:

1. Select the slide on which you want to create a chart.
2. On the **Insert** tab, in the **Illustrations** group, click **Chart.**
3. In the **Insert Chart** dialog box, in left pane, select the type of chart.
4. In the right pane, select the subtype of chart that you want to insert and click **OK.**
5. In the Excel worksheet, make the relevant changes to the data.
6. Close the Excel worksheet.

Procedure Reference: Edit Chart Data

To edit chart data:

1. Click a chart to select it.
2. On the **Design** contextual tab, in the **Data** group, click **Edit Data.**
3. In the Excel worksheet, make the relevant changes to the data.
4. Close the Excel worksheet.

Procedure Reference: Format a Chart

To format a chart:

1. Navigate to the slide that contains the chart you want to format.
2. On the slide, select the chart you want to customize.
3. If necessary, edit the chart data.
4. On the **Layout** contextual tab, in the **Labels** group, from the **Chart Title** drop-down list, select a chart title layout.
5. Select the existing text and type a new title.
6. In the **Labels** group, from the **Legend** drop-down list, select a legend layout for the chart.
7. On the **Layout** contextual tab, in the **Labels** group, from the **Axis Title** drop-down list, select an axis layout for the chart.
8. Click outside the slide to deselect the placeholders.

ACTIVITY 7-1
Creating a Chart

Data Files:

C:\084592Data\Working with Charts\OGC Properties.pptx

Scenario:

You have OGC Properties' performance data for the last four quarters and want to present it in a format that makes it easier to compare and analyze.

Quarter	East	West	North	South
Q1	20	45	45	45
Q2	27	38	46	49
Q3	90	34	70	80
Q4	20	65	43	53

1. Insert a chart.

   a. Navigate to the C:\084592Data\Working with Charts folder and open the OGC Properties.pptx file.

   b. On the **Slides** tab, scroll down and select slide 12.

   c. Select the **Insert** tab, and in the **Illustrations** group, click **Chart.**

   d. In the **Insert Chart** dialog box, in the left pane, verify that **Column** is selected, and in the right pane, verify that the **Clustered Column** chart type, which is the first chart type in the first row, is selected, and click **OK.**

2. Enter data to create a chart.

   a. In the Excel worksheet, in the first row, in the first column, click and type _Quarter_ and press **Tab.**

   b. In the second column, type _East_ and press **Tab.**

   c. In the third column, type _West_ and press **Tab.**

   d. Type _North_

e.   In the fifth column of the first row, click and type *South* and then click in the first column of the second row.

	A	B	C	D	E
					South
1	Quarter	East	West	North	South
2	Category 1	4.3	2.4	2	
3	Category 2	2.5	4.4	2	
4	Category 3	3.5	1.8	3	
5	Category 4	4.5	2.8	5	
6					
7					

(E1 — X ✓ fx South)

f.   In the first column of the second row, click and type *Q1* and press **Tab** and then type *20*

g.   In the third, fourth, and fifth columns of the second row, type *45, 45,* and *47* respectively.

h.   Observe that the changes made to the chart data in the Excel worksheet are reflected in the chart.

i.   Similarly, in the third, fourth, and fifth rows, enter the information from the table in the scenario.

j.   Close the Microsoft Excel 2010 window.

3.   Insert a title for the chart.

a.   Select the **Layout** contextual tab, and in the **Labels** group, from the **Chart Title** drop-down list, select **Above Chart.**

b.   In the text box with the text "Chart Title," triple-click and type *Financial Overview*

4.   Change the location of the legend.

a.   In the **Labels** group, from the **Legend** drop-down list, select **More Legend Options.**

b.   In the **Format Legend** dialog box, verify that the **Legend Options** tab is selected, and in the **Legend Options** section, select the **Top Right** option.

c.   On the slide, observe that the legend has moved to the top right, and in the dialog box, verify that the **Show the legend without overlapping the chart** check box is checked, and click **Close.**

5.   Modify the data in the chart.

a.   Select the **Design** contextual tab, and in the **Data** group, click **Edit Data** to display the chart data in an Excel worksheet.

b.

Click the cell in the second column of the fifth row and type *80*

c.   Click the cell in the fourth column of the fifth row and type *60*

d.   Close the Microsoft Excel 2010 window.

e.   Observe that the values in the respective columns have changed.

f.   Save the presentation as *My OGC Properties* in the PPTX format.

TOPIC B
Modify a Chart

You inserted a chart in a presentation. You must also ensure that the chart type is appropriate to display the type of data you are analyzing. PowerPoint provides you with an option to choose from a wide variety of chart types. In this topic, you will modify a chart.

You may analyze data from a certain perspective, for example, percentage changes over a period of time or relative performance. By choosing the right kind of chart to present data, you will be able to display the relationship of multiple sets of data more clearly to create more visually appealing and engaging presentations.

Chart Layouts

Chart layouts are predefined layout options applied to different chart types. PowerPoint includes a variety of predefined layouts in the **Chart Layout** gallery. These predefined layouts include chart elements such as titles, legends, data tables, and labels. A predefined layout can also be fine-tuned by manually formatting the individual chart elements.

Figure 7-8: *The predefined layout options for charts.*

Chart Styles

Chart styles are predefined styles that match the applied chart type, chart layout, and presentation theme. You can apply a style to an existing chart from the **Chart Styles** group on the **Design** contextual tab.

Format Chart Elements

PowerPoint helps you select and format the desired chart elements from the **Labels** group on the **Layout** contextual tab under the **Chart Tools** tool tab.

Formatting Option	Allows You To
Chart Title	Add, remove, or position the chart title.
Axis Titles	Add, remove, or position the text used to label each axis.
Legend	Add, remove, or position the chart legend.
Data Labels	Add, remove, or position data labels.

Formatting Option	Allows You To
Data Table	Add and remove a data table to the chart.

How to Modify a Chart
Procedure Reference: Change a Chart Type

To change a chart type:
1. Navigate to the slide that contains a chart and click the chart to select it.
2. On the **Chart Tools** tool tab, on the **Design** contextual tab, in the **Type** group, click **Change Chart Type.**
3. In the **Change Chart Type** dialog box, in the left pane, select a chart type.
4. In the right pane, from the displayed chart subtypes, select the desired chart and click **OK.**

Procedure Reference: Change a Chart Style and Layout

To change a chart style and layout:
1. Navigate to the slide that contains the chart for which you want to change the chart layout.
2. On the slide, select the chart.
3. On the **Chart Tools** tool tab, on the **Design** contextual tab, select a chart style.
   - In the **Chart Styles** group, from the displayed gallery, select a style for the chart or;
   - In the **Chart Styles** group, click the **More** button, and from the displayed gallery, select a style.
4. Select a chart layout.
   - In the **Chart Layouts** group, from the displayed gallery, select a layout type or;
   - In the **Chart Layouts** group, click the **More** button, and from the displayed gallery, select a layout type.

Procedure Reference: Modify the Chart Axes and Use Gridlines

To modify the axes in a chart and use gridlines:
1. Navigate to the desired slide and select a chart.
2. On the **Chart Tools** tool tab, on the **Layout** contextual tab, in the **Axes** group, from the **Axes** drop-down list, select the desired option to modify an axis.
   - Select **Primary Horizontal Axis** and select the desired option to change the formatting of the primary horizontal axis.
   - Select **Primary Vertical Axis** and select the desired option to change the formatting of the primary vertical axis.
3. On the **Chart Tools** tool tab, on the **Layout** contextual tab, in the **Axes** group, click **Gridlines** and select the desired option to display or hide the gridlines.
   - Select **Primary Horizontal Gridlines** and select the desired option to turn on or off the gridlines in the primary horizontal axis or;
   - Select **Primary Vertical Gridlines** and select the desired option to turn on or off the gridlines in the primary vertical axis.

Procedure Reference: Format the Chart Wall

To format the chart wall:

1. On the **Chart Tools** tool tab, on the **Layout** contextual tab, in the **Background** group, from the **Chart Wall** drop-down list, select **More Walls Options.**

2. In the **Format Wall** dialog box, on the **Fill** tab, in the right pane, select the desired option to format the chart wall.

3. Click **Close** to close the **Format Wall** dialog box.

Procedure Reference: Format the Chart Floor

To format the chart floor:

1. On the **Chart Tools** tool tab, on the **Layout** contextual tab, in the **Background** group, from the **Chart Floor** drop-down list, select **More Floor Options.**

2. In the **Format Floor** dialog box, on the **Fill** tab, in the right pane, select the desired option to format the chart floor.

3. Click **Close** to close the **Format Floor** dialog box.

Procedure Reference: Apply a Border to a Chart Element

To apply a border to a chart element:

1. Select the chart element for which you want to apply a border.

2. On the **Chart Tools** tool tab, on the **Format** contextual tab, in the **Current Selection** group, verify that the selected chart element is displayed and click **Format Selection.**

3. In the **Format Data Series** dialog box, select the **Border Color** tab and set the desired options.

4. Select the **Border Style** tab, set the desired border options, and click **Close.**

Procedure Reference: Arrange Chart Elements

To arrange chart elements:

1. Select the chart element you want to arrange.

2. On the **Chart Tools** tool tab, on the **Format** contextual tab, in the **Arrange** group, set the desired option.

   - From the **Bring Forward** drop-down list, select an option to bring the chart forward.

   - From the **Send Backward** drop-down list, select an option to move the chart backward.

   - From the **Align** drop-down list, select an option to align the chart on the slide.

Procedure Reference: Apply Effects to Chart Elements

To apply effects to chart elements:

1. Select the chart for which you want to apply effects.

2. Use the options on the **Format** contextual tab to format the chart element as desired.

   - In the **Styles Shape** group, select an option to set the style of the chart element.

   - In the **WordArt Styles** group, select an option to set the WordArt styles for the chart element.

ACTIVITY 7-2
Modifying a Chart Layout

Before You Begin:
The My OGC Properties.pptx file is open.

Scenario:
In your presentation, you have created a chart representing OGC Properties' financial performance. While reviewing it, you feel that the data will be easier to understand if you present it using a different chart type.

---

1. Change the chart type.

    a. On the **Chart Tools** tool tab, on the **Design** contextual tab, in the **Type** group, click **Change Chart Type.**

    b. In the **Change Chart Type** dialog box, in the left pane, verify that the **Column** tab is selected.

    c. In the right pane, in the **Column** section, select the **Clustered Cylinder** chart type, which is the first chart type in the second row, and click **OK.**

    d. Observe that the chart type has changed.

---

2. Modify the chart layout.

    a. On the **Design** contextual tab, in the **Chart Layouts** group, click the **More** button.

    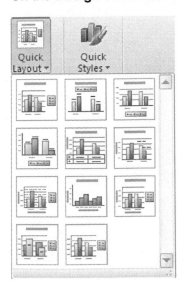

    b. From the displayed gallery, select **Layout7,** which is the first layout in the third row.

    c. Observe that the chart layout has changed.

---

3. Modify the chart style.

a. On the **Design** contextual tab, in the **Chart Styles** group, click the **More** button.

b. From the displayed gallery, select **Style 26,** which is the second style in the fourth row.

c. Observe that the chart style has changed.

d. Save the presentation.

TOPIC C

Import Charts from Other Microsoft Office Applications

You modified a chart in PowerPoint. At times, you may want to reuse a chart from another application to save time. In this topic, you will import a chart from other Microsoft Office applications.

Imagine a situation where you have to use some charts created in Excel. By adding the charts to your presentation with the click of a button, you can save yourself the time and effort needed to re-create them.

How to Import Charts from Other Microsoft Office Applications

Procedure Reference: Copy a Chart from Microsoft Excel

To copy a chart from Microsoft Excel:

1. Open the Excel worksheet that contains a chart.
2. In the worksheet, select the chart and copy it.
   - On the **Home** tab, in the **Clipboard** group, click the **Copy** button or;
   - Press **Ctrl+C.**
3. Switch to the PowerPoint presentation.
4. In the presentation, navigate to the desired slide.
5. On the slide, place the insertion point where you want the chart to appear.
6. Paste the chart on the slide.
   - On the **Home** tab, in the **Clipboard** group, from the **Paste** drop-down list, select **Paste** or;
   - Press **Ctrl+V.**
7. If necessary, click outside the slide to deselect the chart.

 The method to import a chart from Microsoft Word is similar to the steps involved in importing a chart from the Excel application.

ACTIVITY 7-3
Pasting a Chart from Microsoft Excel

Data Files:

C:\084592Data\Working with Charts\Revenue Chart.xlsx

Before You Begin:

1.   The My OGC Properties.pptx file is open.

2.   Open the Microsoft Excel 2010 application.

Scenario:

You received information on the revenue details of your organization in the form of an Excel chart. You want to use the chart in your presentation, but you do not have the time to re-create the chart in PowerPoint. So, you decide to import data from the Excel application into your presentation.

---

1.   Open a worksheet that contains a chart.

   a.   Select the **File** tab and choose **Open**.

   b.   In the **Open** dialog box, navigate to the C:\084592Data\Working with Charts folder.

   c.   Select the **Revenue Chart.xlsx** file and click **Open**.

---

2.   Include the Excel chart in the presentation.

   a.   Select the chart displayed in the worksheet.

   b.   On the **Home** tab, and in the **Clipboard** group, click the **Copy** button.

   c.   Switch to the PowerPoint application.

> If the PowerPoint application window is not fully visible on screen, then maximize the PowerPoint application window.

   d.   On the **Slides** tab, select slide 13.

   e.   On the **Home** tab, in the **Clipboard** group, click **Paste**.

   f.   Observe that the Excel chart is pasted on the slide.

   g.   Align it below the header. This will be done for you.

   h.   Save and close the presentation.

> If necessary, in the **Microsoft Office Excel** message box, click **No** to close the Excel application without saving the changes.

Lesson 7 Follow-up

In this lesson, you added charts to a presentation. Charts enable you to present numerical data in an engaging manner and also enhance the appearance of slides.

1. **List some instances where you might use a chart in a presentation.**

2. **What types of charts do you expect to use most frequently? Why?**

8 | Preparing to Deliver a Presentation

Lesson Time: 45 minutes

Lesson Objectives:

In this lesson, you will prepare to deliver a presentation.

You will:

- Review the content in a presentation.
- Divide a presentation into sections.
- Add transitions.
- Add speaker notes.
- Print a presentation.
- Deliver a presentation.

Introduction

You added charts to a presentation to convey numerical data visually. After creating and editing the presentation, you still need to add final touches to it before delivering it to an audience. In this lesson, you will prepare for delivering a presentation.

Before making or distributing a presentation, you may want to add notes to slides for greater clarity, and to verify that the presentation is accurate and free of any errors. By ensuring that a presentation is correctly sequenced and the information flow is flawless, you can concentrate on making a stellar impression.

TOPIC A
Review the Content in a Presentation

You added a chart to your presentation. Slides, when projected, can magnify small errors in spelling and punctuation. Before you deliver a presentation, you must ensure that the text on the slides is correct. In this topic, you will review the content in a presentation.

Slides filled with spelling and punctuation errors will seriously undermine the credibility of a presentation. By reviewing the content presented on slides, you can ensure that an important presentation is not undermined by careless mistakes.

The Spell Checker Feature

The *Spell Checker* feature allows you to check a presentation for spelling and grammar errors against a built-in word list. The spell checker flags the text, such as proper words or numbers that PowerPoint does not recognize, as errors.

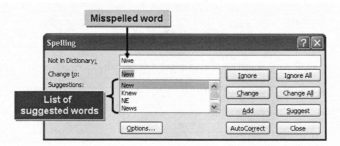

Figure 8-1: The Spelling dialog box.

The **Spelling** dialog box provides you with various options to use and customize the spell checker according to your requirements.

Option	Description
Not in Dictionary	Displays the misspelled text that the spell checker identifies as an error.
Change to	Displays the correct spelling for the word that is displayed in the **Not in Dictionary** text box.
Suggestions	Lists all the possible correct spellings for the word that is displayed in the **Not in Dictionary** text box.
Ignore	Ignores the current occurrence of the misspelled word.
Change	Replaces the current occurrence of the misspelled word with the word selected in the **Suggestions** text box.
Add	Adds the misspelled word to the dictionary. Once it is added to the dictionary, the Spell Checker will not list it as a spelling error.
AutoCorrect	Corrects all the occurrences of the misspelled word that is displayed in the **Not in Dictionary** text box. This will automatically correct the misspelled word across presentations.
Ignore All	Ignores all the occurrences of the misspelled word.

Option	Description
Change All	Replaces all the occurrences of the misspelled word with the word selected in the **Change to** text box.
Suggest	Displays the possible correct option.

The AutoCorrect Feature

AutoCorrect is a feature that automatically fixes common spelling errors as you type. In addition to spelling errors, this feature will automatically capitalize the names of days as well as the first letter of sentences and words. The AutoCorrect list contains a list of often misspelled words and a corresponding list of correct words. You can also add words to the AutoCorrect list to automatically correct them.

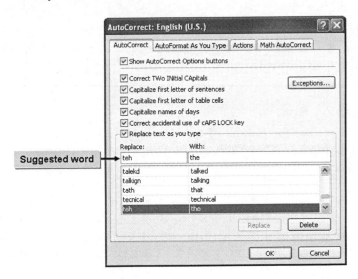

Figure 8-2: The AutoCorrect dialog box.

The AutoCorrect Dialog Box

The *AutoCorrect dialog box* contains a series of tabs that you can use to control the AutoCorrect behavior.

Tab	Description
AutoCorrect	Automatically edit typographical or capitalization errors.
AutoFormat As You Type	Automatically format the text as you type.
Actions	Provides additional actions for certain words or phrases in the presentation through the right-click context menu.
Math AutoCorrect	Automatically replace expressions with the corresponding symbols.

The Research Task Pane

The *Research task pane* allows you to search for information using a wide variety of online references. This pane can be accessed by clicking the **Research** button in the **Proofing** group on the **Review** tab.

Option	Description
The **Search for** text box	Displays the selected word for which a search is initiated. You can also enter the word for which you need to find synonyms and antonyms.
The **Start searching** button	Initiates a search for the word entered in the **Search for** text box.
The **Back** button	Navigates to the previous search results.
The **Next search** button	Navigates to the next word you searched for.
The **Results** list box	Displays the synonyms and antonyms for the selected word.
The **Research options** link	Opens the **Research Options** dialog box that contains numerous options to set research options for the task pane.

The Research Options Dialog Box

The **Research options** link located at the bottom of the **Research** task pane allows you to open the **Research Options** dialog box. Using this dialog box, you can customize the reference books and research sites that you want to access.

The Results List Box

The **Results** list box consists of two links: **All Reference Books** and **All Research Sites.** The **All Reference Books** link directs you to a location from which you can search in a dictionary and the thesaurus, and use the translation option. The **All Research Sites** link checks for synonyms on the web.

The Thesaurus Tool

Thesaurus, a reference tool, provides you with a collection of synonyms and antonyms. To use this feature, you have to select the word for which you want a synonym and click the **Thesaurus** button in the **Proofing** group on the **Review** tab. This displays a list of synonyms and antonyms in the **Research** task pane. By default, synonyms and antonyms are accessed from the Thesaurus English (U.S.) reference book. However, thesauruses are also available in other languages such as French and Spanish.

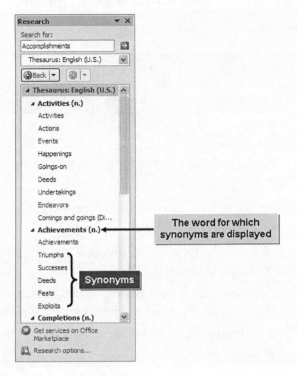

Figure 8-3: *The Thesaurus English (U.S.) reference book.*

How to Review the Content in a Presentation

Procedure Reference: Set the AutoCorrect Options

To set the AutoCorrect options:

1. Select the **File** tab and choose **Options.**
2. In the **PowerPoint Options** dialog box, in the left pane, select **Proofing.**
3. Click the **AutoCorrect Options** button.
4. In the **AutoCorrect** dialog box, set the desired options.

    - Check the **Correct TWo INitial CApitals** check box to change the casing of the second letter of a word to lowercase if the casing of the first two letters of the word is uppercase.

    - Check the **Capitalize first letter of sentences** check box to capitalize the first letter of a sentence.

    - Check the **Capitalize first letter of table cells** check box to capitalize the first letter in a table cell.

    - Check the **Capitalize names of days** check box to capitalize the names of the days of the week.

    - Check the **Correct accidental use Of cAPS LOCK** check box to capitalize the first letter of a word and change the casing of the rest of the letters to lowercase.

    - Check the **Replace text as you type** check box to correct spelling errors as you type.

5. Click **OK** to apply the desired AutoCorrect options.
6. In the **PowerPoint Options** dialog box, click **OK.**

Procedure Reference: Check a Presentation for Spelling Errors

To check a presentation for spelling errors:

 If the insertion point is not at the top of the document, PowerPoint starts the spell check at the location of the insertion point, works to the end of the document and then checks from the beginning of the document to the insertion point.

1. Start the spell checker.
   - On the **Review** tab, in the **Proofing** group, click **Spelling** or;
   - Press **F7.**
2. In the **Spelling** dialog box, use the **Spell Checker** options to correct the spelling errors.
   - Change the spelling.
     - Click **Change,** if the correction that you want to make is already displayed in the **Change to** text box.
     - In the **Suggestions** list box, select the correct word and click **Change,** if the correction that you want to make is not highlighted in the **Suggestions** list box.
     - Click **Change All** to automatically correct all the occurrences of the spelling error in the document.
     - Click **Delete** to delete the second instance of the repeated word.
   - Leave the word unchanged.
     - Click **Ignore** to leave the word unchanged and continue with spell checking the document.
     - Click **Ignore All** to automatically ignore all the remaining occurrences of the word.
   - Add a word to the dictionary.
     - If you want to add a word to the default dictionary, click **Add.** Once it is added to the dictionary, the spell checker will not list it as a spelling error.
   - Stop the spell check.
     - Click **Close** to stop the spell check procedure at any point.
   - Add a word to the AutoCorrect list.
     - Click the **AutoCorrect** button to add a misspelled word and its correct spelling to the AutoCorrect list. Once it is added to the AutoCorrect list, the spell checker will not list it as a spelling error.

 You can also right-click a spelling error and choose the correct spelling.

Procedure Reference: Insert a Synonym by Using the Thesaurus on the Shortcut Menu

To insert a synonym by using the Thesaurus on the shortcut menu:

1. Right-click the word for which you want to find a synonym.
2. Choose **Synonyms** to display a list of words with similar meaning.

3. Choose the desired word to replace the original word.

 If a word is misspelled or unrecognized by PowerPoint, the **Synonyms** option will not be available on the shortcut menu.

Procedure Reference: Insert a Synonym by Using the Thesaurus in the Research Task Pane

To insert a synonym by using the Thesaurus in the **Research** task pane:

1. Select the word for which you want to find the synonyms.
2. Display the Thesaurus in the **Research** task pane.
   - On the **Review** tab, in the **Proofing** group, click **Thesaurus** or;
   - On the **Review** tab, in the **Proofing** group, click **Research** or;
   - Right-click the word that you want to find a synonym for and choose **Synonyms**→ **Thesaurus** or;
   - Press **Shift+F7.**
3. If necessary, in the **Research** task pane, in the list box, scroll to locate the appropriate synonym.
4. In the **Research** task pane, in the list box, place the mouse pointer over the synonym that you want to insert, click the drop-down arrow to the right of the synonym, and select **Insert** to insert the synonym.

ACTIVITY 8-1
Checking a Presentation for Spelling Errors

Data Files:

C:\084592Data\Preparing to Deliver a Presentation\OGC Properties.pptx

Scenario:

You have completed adding content to the presentation that your CEO is going to use. Before sending it for his review, you want to ensure that the presentation is free from spelling errors and typographical mistakes.

---

1. Observe the functionality of the AutoCorrect feature.

    a. Navigate to the C:\084592Data\Preparing to Deliver a Presentation folder and open the OGC Properties.pptx file.

    b. On the **Slides** tab, select slide 18.

    c. On the slide, in the first sentence, click before the text "Services" and type *teh*

    d. Press the **Spacebar.**

    e. Observe that the typed word is automatically corrected to "The."

---

2. Correct the spelling errors in the presentation.

    a. Select the **Review** tab, and in the **Proofing** group, click **Spelling.**

    b. Observe that "OGCBuddy" is displayed as an error in the **Spelling** dialog box because it is not in the main dictionary. In the **Spelling** dialog box, click **Add** to add "OGCBuddy" to the dictionary.

    c. Observe the misspelled word "Acheived" and click **Change** to correct the misspelled word.

    d. In the **Microsoft PowerPoint** message box, click **OK** to acknowledge completion of the spell check process.

    e. Save the presentation as *My OGC Properties* in the PPTX format.

ACTIVITY 8-2
Using the Thesaurus Feature

Before You Begin:
The My OGC Properties.pptx file is open.

Scenario:
You are reviewing your presentation and find that the word "accomplishments" is not appropriate in the phrase "Fiscal Accomplishments" in the title of a slide. You want to replace it with an alternative that fits the context better.

---

1. Display the **Research** task pane.

   a. On the **Slides** tab, verify that slide 14 is selected.

   b. On the slide, double-click the word "Accomplishments" to select it.

   c. On the **Review** tab, in the **Proofing** group, click **Thesaurus** to display the **Research** task pane.

---

2. Replace a word with its synonym by using the Thesaurus.

   a. In the **Research** task pane, in the **Search for** text box, observe that the text "Accomplishments" is displayed.

   b. In the **Research** task pane, in the list box, place the mouse pointer over the word "Achievements," click the drop-down arrow and from the displayed list, select **Insert**.

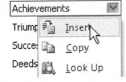

   c. Observe that the title now reads "Fiscal Achievements."

   d. Close the **Research** task pane.

   e. Save the presentation.

TOPIC B
Divide a Presentation into Sections

You reviewed the content in a presentation. You may also want to apply further customizing options such as grouping slides into identifiable sections so that you can organize the presentation. In this topic, you will divide a presentation into sections.

Imagine a situation where you had to prepare a presentation that includes content on half a dozen subjects or more. Without segregating similar slides into groups, finding a particular slide to edit, will become a time-consuming task. This is particularly annoying when you do not have much time at hand. PowerPoint 2010 provides you with the option of grouping related slides into sections, so that you can quickly identify the slides that you need.

The Slide Section Feature

The Slide Section feature that can be accessed from the **Slides** group on the **Home** tab enables you to organize slides in a presentation into sections. You can name sections to track various groups of slides that belong to a category. You can also rename, move, and remove a section based on your needs.

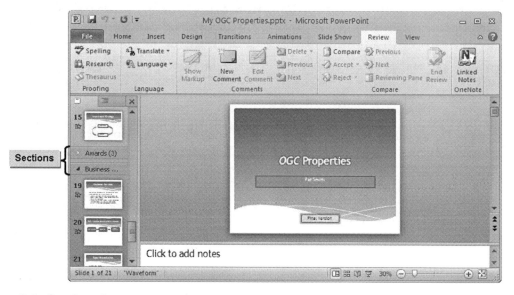

Figure 8-4: Sections in a presentation.

How to Divide a Presentation into Sections

Procedure Reference: Create a Slide Section

To create a slide section:

1. Select the slide from which you want to create a new section.

2. Add a section.

   - On the **Home** tab, in the **Slides** group, from the **Section** drop-down list, select **Add Section** or;

   - Right-click between the two slides where you want to add a section and choose **Add Section.**

3. Observe that an **Untitled Section** is added to the left pane.

4. Rename the section.

   - Right-click **Untitled Section** and select **Rename Section.**

   - On the **Home** tab, in the **Slides** group, click **Section** and choose **Rename Section.**

5. In the **Rename Section** dialog box, in the **Section name** text box, type a name and click **Rename.**

6. If necessary, reorganize slides using sections.

   - Right-click a section and select **Move Section Down** to move it after the section that follows it.

   - Right-click a section and select **Move Section Up** to move it before the preceding section.

7. If necessary, drag a slide onto the relevant section to include it in that section.

ACTIVITY 8-3
Dividing a Presentation

Before You Begin:

The My OGC Properties.pptx file is open.

Scenario:

Your presentation has multiple slides. The CEO wants to recognize staff performances and announce special awards during the presentation and has asked you to present only the main part. You want to categorize slides to quickly identify the portions that you both need to present.

1. Create sections for the "Sales Overview" and "Awards" slides.

   a. On the **Slides** tab, right-click between slides 8 and 9 and choose **Add Section.**

   b. Observe that an **Untitled Section** is added between slides 8 and 9.

   c. On the **Slides** group, right-click **Section** and choose **Rename Section.**

   d. In the **Rename Section** dialog box, in the **Section name** text box, type *Business Overview* and click **Rename.**

   e. Click between slides 18 and 19.

   f. Select the **Home** tab, and in the **Slides** group, click **Section** and choose **Add Section.**

   g. On the **Home** tab, in the **Slides** group, click **Section** and choose **Rename Section.**

   h. In the **Rename Section** dialog box, in the **Section name** text box, type *Awards* and click **Rename.**

2. Reorder the sections and slides.

   a. Right-click the **Business Overview** section and select **Move Section Down** to move the section below the **Awards** section.

   b. Observe that the sections are now displayed as desired.

   c. On the **Slides** tab, click slide 20 and drag it below slide 9. This will be done for you.

   d. Save the presentation.

TOPIC C

Add Transitions

You created sections to organize slides in a presentation. After dividing the presentation into relevant sections, you may want to add visually attractive effects to switch between slides. In this topic, you will add transitions between slides.

By adding visual effects when switching between slides, you can enhance a presentation and ensure a smooth movement from one slide to the next. By adding transitions, you can also control the pace at which slides change.

Transitions

Definition:

Transitions are special effects that appear while advancing slides in a slide show. A star appears under the slide number on the **Slides** tab to indicate that a transition effect is applied to that slide. You can change the transition speed and add sounds to slide transitions. You can also change or remove the existing transitions applied to slides in a presentation. Transitions can occur on a mouse click or key press, or be set to appear automatically after a specified period of time during a slide show.

Example:

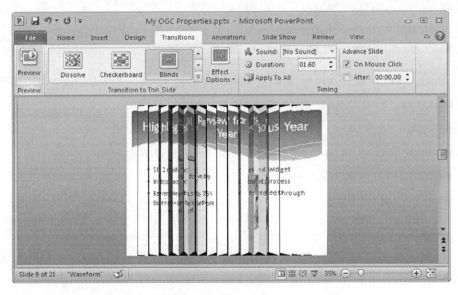

Figure 8-5: A transition effect in PowerPoint 2010.

How to Add Transitions

Procedure Reference: Add Transition Effects

To add transition effects:

1. Select the slide to which you want to add a transition.

2. On the Ribbon, select the **Transitions** tab.

3. Apply a transition.

   - In the **Transition to This Slide** group, select a transition or;

   - In the **Transition to This Slide** group, click the **More** button, and from the displayed gallery of transitions, select a transition.

4. If necessary, in the **Timing** group, specify the desired options.

   - In the **Timing** group, click **Apply To All** to apply the transition effect to all the slides in the presentation.

   - In the **Timing** group, from the **Duration** spin box, select the duration for which the transition should occur.

   - In the **Timing** group, from the **Sound** drop-down list, select a sound to play along with the transition.

5. Select the **Slide Show** tab, and in the **Start Slide Show** group, select the desired option to view the slide transitions in a slide show.

   - Click **From Beginning** to start the slide show from the first slide.

   - Click **From Current Slide** to start the slide show from the current slide.

6. End the slide show.

   - Right-click the slide and choose **End Show** or:

   - Press **Esc.**

Procedure Reference: Change Transition Effects

To change transition effects:

1. Select the slides for which you want to change the transition.

2. On the Ribbon, select the **Transitions** tab.

3. Change the existing transition effects.

   - On the **Transitions** tab, in the **Transition to This Slide** group, click the **More** button, and from the displayed gallery of transitions, select a transition.

   - In the **Transition to This Slide** group, in the **Duration** spin box, set the slide transition duration.

   - In the **Transition to This Slide** group, from the **Sound** drop-down list, select a sound to add a transition sound.

4. If necessary, in the **Timing** group, click **Apply To All** to change the transition effect for all the slides in the presentation.

5. Run the presentation to view the transition effects.

Procedure Reference: Remove Transition Effects

To remove transition effects:

1. Select the slides for which you want to remove the transition.

2. On the Ribbon, select the **Transitions** tab.

3. Remove the existing transition effects.

   ● In the **Transition to This Slide** group, click the **More** button, and from the displayed gallery, select **None.**

   ● In the **Transition to This Slide** group, from the **Sound** drop-down list, select the **No Sound** option.

4. Run the presentation to verify that the transition effects are removed.

ACTIVITY 8-4
Adding Transition Effects to a Presentation

Before You Begin:

The My OGC Properties.pptx file is open.

Scenario:

To make the presentation interesting to the audience, you decide to add visually captivating transition effects between slides. This will make the switch between slides more appealing.

---

1. Apply the **Dissolve** transition effect for a duration of one second.

    a. On the **Slides** tab, select slide 1.

    b. Select the **Transitions** tab, and in the **Transition to This Slide** group, click the **More** button, and from the displayed gallery, in the **Exciting** section, select the **Dissolve** transition, which is the first transition in the first row.

    c. Observe the transition that is applied to the slide.

    d. In the **Timing** group, in the **Duration** spin box, click the down arrow to set the slide transition duration to 01.00.

---

2. Apply the transition effect to other slides in the presentation.

    a. In the **Timing** group, click **Apply To All.**

    b. On the **Slides** tab, observe that a star icon is present to the left of each slide confirming that a transition effect is applied to them.

    c. On the **Slides** tab, select slide 5.

    d. Select the **Slide Show** tab, and in the **Start Slide Show** group, click **From Current Slide.**

    e. Observe that the current slide is displayed in the Slide Show view. Click anywhere on the presentation screen to view the slide transition and display the next slide.

    f. Right-click on the slide and choose **End Show** to exit the slide show.

    g. Save the presentation.

TOPIC D
Add Speaker Notes

You added transition effects to a presentation. You now need to prepare hints and pointers to help you explain the content during a presentation. In this topic, you will add speaker notes for the slides in a presentation.

A PowerPoint presentation becomes effective only if it conveys all the essential information. However, while delivering a presentation, there is a possibility that the presenter may forget some of the key points that were intended to be conveyed. Adding speaker notes keeps the slides free of clutter and too much information, and also helps the presenter recollect the points to be presented.

Speaker Notes

Speaker notes are support materials that can be printed for the presenter to refer to during a presentation. Speaker notes are displayed in the Notes text area below the slide image in the Notes Page view. This information can be added in the Notes Page view as well as the Normal view. The Notes page view may be preferred for entering text because in this view you can add headers and footers, as well as resize slide images. Text in the Notes text area can be formatted with the basic font and paragraph formatting commands. When you print the Notes pages, the slide image along with the information you entered in the Notes text area is printed.

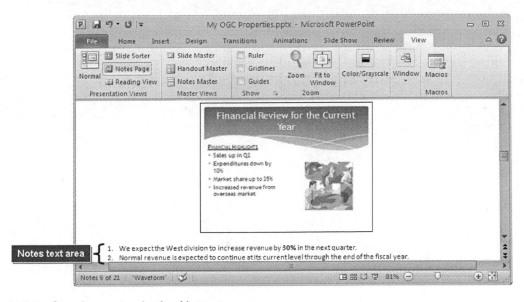

Figure 8-6: Speaker notes in the Notes pane.

How to Add Speaker Notes

Procedure Reference: Add Speaker Notes to Slides in the Normal View

To add speaker notes to slides in the Normal view:

1. In the left pane, on the **Slides** tab, select the slide for which you want to add notes.
2. In the **Notes** pane at the bottom of the screen, click and type your notes.
3. If necessary, format the notes.

Procedure Reference: Add Speaker Notes to Slides in the Notes Page View

To add speaker notes to slides in the Notes Page view:

1. On the **View** tab, in the **Presentation Views** group, click **Notes Page.**
2. In the Notes Page view, navigate to the slide for which you want to add notes.
3. In the Notes Page view, click the **Click to add text** placeholder and type your notes.
4. If necessary, format the notes.

ACTIVITY 8-5
Adding Speaker Notes

Before You Begin:

The My OGC Properties.pptx file is open.

Scenario:

Your presentation contains financial information and a brief comparative analysis of sales data across various divisions. You are comfortable with the slides that contain mostly text, but on the slides with charts and graphs, you want to add some reminders of the important points.

1. Type the notes.

   a. On the **Slides** tab, select slide 17.

   b. Select the **View** tab, and in the **Presentation Views** group, click **Notes Page**.

   c. In the Notes Page view, click the **Click to add text** placeholder and type *We expect the West division to increase revenue by 30% in the next quarter.* Then, press **Enter.**

   d. Type *North division revenue is expected to continue at its current level through the end of the fiscal year.*

2. Format the notes.

   a. Select the **Home** tab, and in the **Editing** group, from the **Select** drop-down list, select **Select All** to select all the text in the **Notes** section.

   b. In the **Paragraph** group, click the **Numbering** button.

   c. Deselect the text.

   d. Click and drag over 30% to select the text "30%."

   e. In the **Font** group, click the **Bold** button to apply bold formatting.

   f. Save the presentation.

TOPIC E
Print a Presentation

You added speaker notes to the slides. Speaker notes will serve as a reference for the presenter when delivering a presentation. However, if you intend to provide hard copies of the presentation for your audience, you need to print it. In this topic, you will print a presentation.

Having a hard copy of the presentation will help you refer to the presentation you delivered, when you do not have access to a computer. Also, providing hard copies of the presentation to the audience will allow them to refer to the content you are presenting, jot down notes, and increase their ability to remember the content of your presentation better.

The Print Option

The **Print** option in PowerPoint is integrated in the Backstage view. It is divided into two panes. The left pane is used to specify print options and printer settings, while the right pane displays a preview of the presentation. The right pane also contains the **Zoom** slider and options to view the next and previous pages.

The left pane in the **Print** option allows you to specify various options for printing a presentation.

Left Pane Section	Enables You To
Print	Set the number of copies that need to be printed and print a presentation.
Printer	Select a printer from the list of available printers.
Settings	Specify the range of pages that need to be printed, set the page orientation, select a paper size, and set margin properties.

Handouts

Handouts are support materials that can be used by the audience to make notes during a presentation. Usually, the date of the presentation and the page number are printed on the handouts for reference. You can also generate handouts by creating separate documents that display slides. The **Save & Send** section in the Backstage view allows you to create handouts in Microsoft Word.

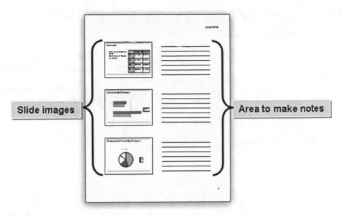

Figure 8-7: *The print preview of handouts.*

Outlines

Outlines are printed support materials that contain all the text on each slide in a condensed format. Slide numbers are also visible in outlines; however, graphics and other objects do not appear. You can print outlines and provide the audience with a printed copy of text that is used on slides, which they can reference while viewing the presentation.

Figure 8-8: *The outline of a presentation.*

The Page Setup Dialog Box

The **Page Setup** dialog box contains various options to modify the overall layout of a slide by setting the size and orientation. You can specify the width and height of a slide in the **Width** and **Height** spin boxes, respectively. You can also determine the numbering of slides by setting a starting number in the **Number slides from** spin box. In the **Slides** section, you can set the page orientation to either *Portrait* or *Landscape*. In the **Notes, handouts & outline** section, you can choose an orientation for notes, handouts, and outlines. This orientation can be different from the one that you chose for the slides.

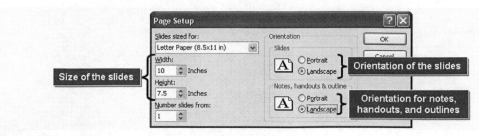

Figure 8-9: Options in the Page Setup dialog box.

Page Orientation

Page orientation is the way in which a rectangular page is oriented for normal viewing. The two types of orientation are **Portrait** and **Landscape.** These options can be accessed by clicking the **Slide Orientation** button on the **Design** tab in the **Page Setup** group or in the **Page Setup** dialog box. In **Portrait** orientation, the height of the display area is greater than the width, while in **Landscape,** orientation, the width of the display area is greater than the height.

How to Print a Presentation

Procedure Reference: Preview a Presentation

To preview a presentation:

1. Select the **File** tab and choose **Print.**
2. In the right pane, preview the selected slide.
3. In the preview section, at the bottom-left corner, click the left and right arrow buttons to navigate and preview other slides in the presentation.

Procedure Reference: Create Handouts in Microsoft Word

To create handouts in Microsoft Word:

1. On the **File** tab, select the **Save & Send** option.
2. In the **File Types** section, select **Create Handouts.**
3. In the right pane, in the **Create Handouts in Microsoft Word** section, click **Create Handouts.**
4. In the **Send To Microsoft Word** dialog box, select a layout for the handouts document, select an option for pasting the slide content on the handouts document, and click **OK.**
5. In the Word document, view the contents of the handout.
6. On the Quick Access toolbar, click **Save.**
7. In the **Save As** dialog box, navigate to the location where you want to save the document.
8. If necessary, from the **Save as type** drop-down list, select the desired file format.
9. In the **File name** text box, type the name of the file.
10. Click **Save.**

Procedure Reference: Print Slides, Handouts, Notes, or Outlines

To print slides, handouts, notes, or outlines:

1. On the **Design** tab, in the **Page Setup** group, click the **Page Setup** button.
2. In the **Page Setup** dialog box, set the page size and orientation.
   - Set the page size.

- From the **Slides sized for** drop-down list, select the size of the paper for printing.
- In the **Width** and **Height** text boxes, enter the required width and height values to customize the page size.
- In the **Notes, handouts & outline** section, select the desired orientation.

 Page orientation options can also be set by using the **Slide Orientation** drop-down list in the **Page Setup** group on the **Design** tab.

3. Display the **Print** dialog box.
   - Select the **File** tab, choose **Print,** and click the **Print** button or;
   - Press **Ctrl+P.**
4. Click **OK.**
5. If necessary, from the **Printer** drop-down list, select the name of the printer to which you want to print.
6. If necessary, in the **Settings** section, select an option for printing the slides.
   - Select the options for printing the entire presentation, the current slide, or a custom range.
   - In the **Slides** text box, enter the range of slides to print specified slides of the presentation.
7. If necessary, in the **Print** section, in the **Copies** spin box, enter the number of copies you want to print.
8. If necessary, below the **Slides** text box, click the **Full Page Slides** drop-down arrow and select a printout type.
   - In the **Print Layout** section, select the layout that you want to print.
   - If necessary, in the **Handouts** section, select the number of slides that you want to print on each page.
9. If necessary, from the **Color** drop-down list, select a print output option.
   - Select the **Color** option to print in color.
   - Select the **Grayscale** option to print images that contain variations of gray tones between black and white.
   - Select the **Pure Black and White** option to print a handout with no gray fills.
10. In the **Print** section, click **Print** to print the presentation.

ACTIVITY 8-6
Printing a Presentation

Before You Begin:

The My OGC Presentation.pptx file is open.

Scenario:

Your presentation is ready for delivery. You want to print a copy of the presentation for the company project history file which could be used by the CEO for future reference. You want only the titles and text from each slide on the printout for reference.

---

1. Set the slide orientation and page size for the presentation.

    a. Select the **Design** tab, and in the **Page Setup** group, click **Page Setup.**

    b. In the **Page Setup** dialog box, in the **Slides** section, verify that **Landscape** is selected.

    c. In the **Notes, handouts & outline** section, select **Landscape.**

    d. From the **Slides sized for** drop-down list, select **Letter Paper (8.5x11 in).**

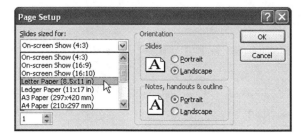

    e. Click **OK** to apply the page settings to the presentation.

---

2. Print an outline of the presentation.

    a. Select the **File** tab and choose **Print.**

b. In the **Settings** section, click the **Full Page Slides** button, and in the **Print Layout** section, select **Outline.**

c. In the right pane, preview the outline, and in the **Print** section, click **Print.**

d. Save the presentation.

e. Select the **View** tab, and in the **Presentation Views** group, click **Normal.**

ACTIVITY 8-7
Printing Speaker Notes and Handouts

Before You Begin:

The My OGC Properties.pptx file is open.

Scenario:

Your presentation is now ready for delivery. You decide to deliver your presentation along with brief descriptions on the data being presented. For the CEO's reference, you want to print the notes associated with the slides. You are also informed that your presentation is going to be included as an appendix in the annual report. So, you need to print the handouts too.

---

1. Print the speaker notes for slide 13.

    a. Select the **File** tab and choose **Print.**

    b. In the **Settings** section, click the **Full Page Slides** button, and in the **Print Layout** section, select **Notes Pages.**

    c. In the **Settings** section, in the **Slides** text box, click and type *13*

    d. Click **Print** to print the notes.

---

2. Print three handouts per page.

    a. Select the **File** tab and choose **Print.**

    b. In the **Settings** section, from the **Custom Range** drop-down list, select **Print All Slides** to print all the slides as handouts.

    c. From the **Full Page Slides** drop-down list, in the **Handouts** section, select **3 Slides.**

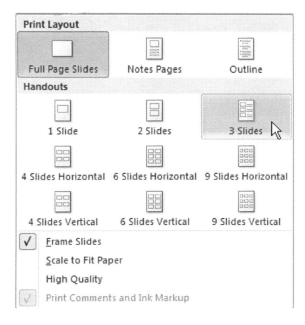

d.   In the right pane, preview the slide handouts.

e.   Click **Print.**

f.   Select the **View** tab, and in the **Presentation Views** group, click **Normal.**

g.   Save the presentation.

TOPIC F
Deliver a Presentation

You printed a presentation and handed out the reference materials to your audience. The final task after creating the entire presentation is to deliver it to an audience. In this topic, you will deliver a presentation.

After the entire creating, editing, and formatting processes, the final task left is to display the presentation on a big screen. PowerPoint provides you with various options to make presentation delivery a memorable experience both for the presenter as well as for the audience.

How to Deliver a Presentation

Procedure Reference: Deliver a Presentation

To deliver a presentation:

1. Display a presentation in any desired presentation view.
2. If necessary, hide the slides.
    *   In the left pane, right-click the desired slide and choose **Hide Slide** or;
    *   Select the desired slide, and on the **Slide Show** tab, in the **Set Up** group, click **Hide Slide.**
3. Display the presentation in the Slide Show view.
    *   On the **Slide Show** tab, in the **Start Slide Show** group, select the desired option for viewing the slides or;
        *   Select **From Beginning** to view the slide show from the beginning.
        *   Select **From Current Slide** to view the slide show from the current slide.
        *   Select **Broadcast Slide Show** to broadcast the slide show on the web.
        *   Select **Custom Slide Show** to display only selected slides.
    *   On the status bar, select **Slide Show** or;
    *   Press **F5.**
4. If necessary, click the screen to advance to the next slide in the presentation.
5. End the slide show.
    *   Press **Esc.**
    *   Right-click the slide and choose **End Show.**

ACTIVITY 8-8
Delivering a Presentation

Before You Begin:
The My OGC Properties.pptx file is open.

Scenario:
While doing a final review, the CEO feels that certain slides are redundant and need not be viewed by the audience. So, you decide to hide them.

---

1. Hide slide 4 in the presentation.

    a. On the **Slides** tab, select slide 4.

    b. Select the **Slide Show** tab, and in the **Set Up** group, click **Hide Slide.**

---

2. Deliver the presentation.

    a. On the **Slides** tab, select slide 3.

    b. In the **Start Slide Show** group, click **From Current Slide** to view the slide show from slide 3.

    c. Click the slide to advance to the next slide in the presentation.

    d. Observe that the Our Goal slide is displayed after the Agenda slide. Also observe that the About Us slide, which is the fourth slide of the presentation was not displayed because it is hidden.

    e. Right-click the slide and choose **End Show.**

    f. Save the presentation and close it.

    g. Close the PowerPoint application.

Lesson 8 Follow-up

In this lesson, you prepared to deliver a presentation. You can now be confident in delivering a professional presentation.

1. **What benefits do you see in using the spell checker and research tools in a presentation?**

2. **What is the difference between transition effects that enhance your presentation versus transition effects that could detract from your presentation?**

Follow-up

In this course, you explored the PowerPoint environment and then created a presentation. You formatted the text on slides to enhance clarity. To enhance the visual appeal, you added graphical objects to the presentation and modified them. You also added tables and charts to the presentation to display data in a structured form. You then finalized a presentation to deliver it.

1. **As you create presentations in PowerPoint, which elements (text, graphics, tables, charts, animation) will you make the most use of?**

2. **How will PowerPoint assist you in getting your information and ideas across to your audience more effectively than other methods?**

3. **Where might you become more efficient in creating your current presentations by using the new features in PowerPoint 2010?**

What's Next?

Microsoft® Office PowerPoint® 2010: Level 2 is the next course in this series. In that course, you will use Microsoft Office PowerPoint 2010 features to draw, animate, and format presentations with professional-quality content so that they may be communicated to a wide variety of live, remote, and self-service audiences.

A | Microsoft Office PowerPoint 2010 Exam 77–883

Selected Element K courseware addresses Microsoft Office Specialist certification skills for Microsoft Office 2010. The following table indicates where PowerPoint 2010 skills are covered. For example, 3-A indicates the lesson and topic number applicable to that skill, and 3-1 indicates the lesson and activity number.

Objective Domain	Level	Topic	Activity
1. Managing the PowerPoint Environment			
1.1. Adjust views			
1.1.1 Adjust views by using ribbon	1	1-B	1-2
1.1.2 Adjust views by status bar commands	1	1-A	
1.2. Manipulate the PowerPoint window			
1.2.1 Work with multiple presentation windows simultaneously	2	1-A	
1.3. Configure the Quick Access Toolbar			
1.3.1 Show the Quick Access Toolbar (QAT) below the ribbon	2	1-A	1-1
1.4. Configure PowerPoint file options			
1.4.1 Use PowerPoint Proofing	1	8-A	8-1
1.4.2 Use PowerPoint Save options	2	1-B	1-2
2. Creating a Slide Presentation			
2.1. Construct and edit photo albums			
2.1.1. Add captions to picture	1	4-A	
2.1.2. Insert text	1	4-A	
2.1.3. Insert images in black and white	1	4-A	
2.1.4. Reorder pictures in an album	1	4-A	
2.1.5. Adjust image			
2.1.5.1. Rotation	1	4-A	
2.1.5.2. Brightness	1	4-A	
2.1.5.3. Contrast	1	4-A	

Objective Domain	Level	Topic	Activity
2.2. Apply slide size and orientation settings			
2.2.1. Set up a custom size	1	8-E	8-6
2.2.2. Change the orientation	1	8-E	8-6
2.3. Add and remove slides			
2.3.1. Insert an outline	1	2-E	
2.3.2. Reuse slides from a saved presentation	1	2-E	2-5
2.3.3. Reuse slides from a slide library	2	6-B	
2.3.4. Duplicate selected slides	1	2-E	
2.3.5. Delete multiple slides simultaneously	1	2-F	
2.3.6. Include non-contiguous slides in a presentation	2	5-A	
2.4. Format slides			
2.4.1. Format sections	2	2-A	2-1
2.4.2. Modify themes	1	2-G	2-7
2.4.3. Switch to a different slide layout	2	2-A	
2.4.4. Apply a formatting to a slide			
2.4.4.1. Fill color	1	2-G	
2.4.4.2. Gradient	1	2-G	
2.4.4.3. Picture	1	2-G	
2.4.4.4. Texture	1	2-G	
2.4.4.5. Pattern	1	2-G	
2.4.5. Set up slide footers	2	2-C	2-3
2.5. Enter and format text			
2.5.1. Use text effects	1	3-A	3-1
2.5.2. Change text format			
2.5.2.1. Indentation	1	3-B	3-2
2.5.2.2. Alignment	1	3-B	
2.5.2.3. Line spacing	1	3-B	3-2
2.5.2.4. Direction	1	3-B	
2.5.3. Change the formatting of bulleted and numbered lists	1	3-B	3-2
2.5.4. Enter text in a placeholder text box	1	2-A	2-1
2.5.5. Convert text to SmartArt	2	3-A	3-2
2.5.6. Copy and pasting text	1	2-C	2-3
2.5.7. Use Paste Special	1	2-C	2-3
2.5.8. Use Format Painter	1	3-A	3-1
2.6. Format text boxes			
2.6.1. Apply formatting to a text box			
2.6.1.1. Fill color	1	2-D	2-4
2.6.1.2. Gradient	1	2-D	

Objective Domain	Level	Topic	Activity
2.6.1.3. Picture	1	2-D	
2.6.1.4. Texture	1	2-D	2-4
2.6.1.5. Pattern	1	2-D	
2.6.2. Change the outline of a text box			
2.6.2.1. Color	1	2-D	2-4
2.6.2.2. Weight	1	2-D	
2.6.2.3. Style	1	2-D	
2.6.3. Change the shape of the text box	1	2-D	
2.6.4. Apply effects	1	2-D	2-4
2.6.5. Set the alignment	1	3-B	
2.6.6. Create columns in a text box	1	3-B	3-2
2.6.7. Set internal margins	1	2-D	
2.6.8. Set the current text box formatting as the default for new text boxes	1	2-D	
2.6.9. Adjust text in a text box			
2.6.9.1. Wrap	1	3-B	
2.6.9.2. Size	1	2-B	
2.6.9.3. Position	1	2-B	
2.6.10. Use AutoFit	1	3-B	
3. Working with Graphical and Multimedia Elements			
3.1. Manipulate graphical elements			
3.1.1. Arrange graphical elements	1	5-E	5-5
3.1.2. Position graphical elements	1	5-D	5-5
3.1.3. Resize graphical elements	1	5-A	5-1
3.1.4. Apply effects to graphical elements	1	5-B	
3.1.5. Apply styles to graphical elements	1	5-B	
3.1.6. Apply borders to graphical elements	1	5-B	
3.1.7. Add hyperlinks to graphical elements	2	5-A	5-1
3.2. Manipulate images			
3.2.1. Apply color adjustments	1	5-B	
3.2.2. Apply image corrections			
3.2.2.1. Sharpen	1	5-B	
3.2.2.2. Soften	1	5-B	
3.2.2.3. Brightness	1	5-B	
3.2.2.4. Contrast	1	5-B	
3.2.3. Add artistic effects to an image	1	5-B	
3.2.4. Remove a background	1	5-A	5-1
3.2.5. Crop a picture	1	5-A	
3.2.6. Compress selected pictures or all pictures	1	5-A	5-1

Objective Domain	Level	Topic	Activity
3.2.7. Change a picture	1	5-B	
3.2.8. Reset a picture	1	5-B	
3.3. Modify WordArt and shapes			
3.3.1. Set the formatting of the current shape as the default for future shapes	1	4-B	
3.3.2. Change the fill color or texture	1	4-C	
3.3.3. Change the WordArt	1	4-C	
3.3.4. Convert Word Art to SmartArt	2	3-A	3-1
3.4. Manipulate SmartArt			
3.4.1. Add and remove shapes	2	4-B	
3.4.2. Change SmartArt styles	2	4-C	
3.4.3. Change the SmartArt layout	2	3-A	
3.4.4. Reorder shapes	2	3-B	
3.4.5. Convert a SmartArt graphic to text	2	3-B	
3.4.6. Convert SmartArt to shapes	2	3-B	
3.4.7. Make shapes larger or smaller	2	3-B	
3.4.8. Promote bullet levels	2	3-B	
3.4.9. Demote bullet levels	2	3-B	
3.5. Edit video and audio content			
3.5.1. Apply a style to video or audio content	2	4-A	
3.5.2. Adjust video or audio content	2	4-A	
3.5.3. Arrange video or audio content	2	4-A	
3.5.4. Size video or audio content	2	4-A	
3.5.5. Adjust playback options	2	4-A	
4. Creating Charts and Tables			
4.1. Construct and modify tables			
4.1.1. Draw a table	1	6-A	
4.1.2. Insert a Microsoft Excel spreadsheet	1	6-C	
4.1.3. Set table style options	1	6-B	6-2
4.1.4. Add shading	1	6-B	
4.1.5. Add borders	1	6-B	
4.1.6. Add effects	1	6-B	
4.1.7. Columns and Rows			
4.1.7.1. Change the alignment	1	6-B	
4.1.7.2. Resize	1	6-B	
4.1.7.3. Merge	1	6-B	
4.1.7.4. Split	1	6-B	
4.1.7.5. Distribute	1	6-B	
4.1.7.6. Arrange	1	6-B	
4.2. Insert and modify charts	1		

Objective Domain	Level	Topic	Activity
4.2.1. Select a chart type	1	7-A	7-1
4.2.2. Enter chart data	1	7-A	7-1
4.2.3. Change the chart type	1	7-B	7-2
4.2.4. Change the chart layout	1	7-B	7-2
4.2.5. Switch row and column	1	7-A	
4.2.6. Select data	1	7-A	
4.2.7. Edit data	1	7-A	7-1
4.3. Apply chart elements.			
4.3.1. Use chart labels	1	7-A	7-1
4.3.2. Use axes	1	7-A	
4.3.3. Use gridlines	1	7-B	
4.3.4. Use backgrounds	1	7-B	
4.4. Manipulate chart layouts			
4.4.1. Select chart elements	1	7-B	
4.4.2. Format selections	1	7-B	
4.5. Manipulate chart elements			
4.5.1. Arrange chart elements	1	7-B	
4.5.2. Specify a precise position	1	7-B	
4.5.3. Apply effects	1	7-B	
4.5.4. Resize chart elements	1	7-B	
4.5.5. Apply Quick Styles	1	7-B	
4.5.6. Apply a border	1	7-B	
4.5.7. Add hyperlinks	2	5-A	
5. Applying Transitions and Animations			
5.1. Apply built-in and custom animations			
5.1.1. Use More Entrance	2	4-B	
5.1.2. Use More Emphasis	2	4-B	
5.1.3. Use More Exit effects	2	4-B	
5.1.4. Use More Motion paths	2	4-B	4-2
5.2. Apply effect and path options			
5.2.1. Set timing	2	4-B	4-2
5.2.2. Set start options	2	4-B	4-2
5.3. Manipulate animations			
5.3.1. Change the direction of an animation	2	4-B	
5.3.2. Attach a sound to an animation	2	4-B	
5.3.3. Use Animation Painter	1	5-E	
5.3.4. Reorder animation	2	4-B	
5.3.5. Selecting text options	2	4-B	
5.4. Apply and modify transitions between slides			
5.4.1. Modifying a transition effect	1	8-C	8-3

Objective Domain	Level	Topic	Activity
5.4.2. Adding a sound to a transition	1	8-C	
5.4.3. Modify transition duration	1	8-C	8-4
5.4.4. Set up manual or automatically timed advance options	2	5-C	5-6
6. Collaborating on Presentations			
6.1. Manage comments in presentations			
6.1.1. Insert and edit comments	2	6-A	6-1
6.1.2. Show or hide markup	2	6-A	
6.1.3. Move to the previous or next comment	2	6-A	
6.1.4. Delete comments	2	6-A	
6.2. Apply proofing tools			
6.2.1. Use Spelling and Thesaurus features	1	8-A	8-1, 8-2
6.2.2. Compare and combine presentations	2	6-A	6-1
7. Preparing Presentations for Delivery			
7.1. Save presentations			
7.1.1. Save the presentation as a picture presentation	1	1-C	
7.1.2. Save the presentation as a PDF	1	1-C	
7.1.3. Save the presentation as a XPS	1	1-C	
7.1.4. Save the presentation as a outline	1	1-C	
7.1.5. Save the presentation as an OpenDocument	1	1-C	
7.1.6. Save the presentation as a show (.ppsx)	1	1-C	
7.1.7. Save a slide or object as a picture file	1	1-C	
7.2. Share presentations			
7.2.1. Package a presentation for CD delivery	2	7-C	7-3
7.2.2. Create video	2	7-B	7-2
7.2.3. Create handouts	1	8-E	8-7
7.2.4. Compress media	2	7-E	7-5
7.3. Print presentations			
7.3.1. Adjust print settings	1	8-E	8-7
7.4. Protect presentations			
7.4.1. Set a password	2	7-E	7-5
7.4.2. Change a password	2	7-E	
7.4.3. Mark a presentation as final	2	7-E	
8. Delivering Presentations			
8.1. Apply presentation tools			
8.1.1. Add pen and highlighter annotations	2	5-B	5-5
8.1.2. Change the ink color	2	5-B	
8.1.3. Erase an annotation	2	5-B	5-5
8.1.4. Discard annotations upon closing	2	5-B	

Objective Domain	Level	Topic	Activity
8.1.5. Retain annotations upon closing	2	5-B	
8.2. Set up slide shows			
8.2.1. Set up a Slide Show	2	5-A	5-1
8.2.2. Play narrations	2	5-C	
8.2.3. Set up Presenter view	2	5-A	
8.2.4. Use timings	2	5-C	5-6
8.2.5. Show media controls	2	4-A	4-1
8.2.6. Broadcast presentations	2	7-A	7-1
8.2.7. Create a Custom Slide Show	2	5-A	5-1
8.3. Set presentation timing			
8.3.1. Rehearse timings	2	5-C	5-6
8.3.2. Keep timings	2	5-C	5-6
8.3.3. Adjust a slide's timing	2	5-C	
8.4. Record presentations			
8.4.1. Starting recording from the beginning of a slide show	2	5-C	
8.4.2. Starting recording from the current slide of the slide show	2	5-C	

Lesson Labs

Lesson labs are provided as an additional learning resource for this course. The labs may or may not be performed as part of the classroom activities. Your instructor will consider setup issues, classroom timing issues, and instructional needs to determine which labs are appropriate for you to perform, and at what point during the class. If you do not perform the labs in class, your instructor can tell you if you can perform them independently as self-study, and if there are any special setup requirements.

Lesson 1 Lab 1

Getting Started with PowerPoint

Activity Time: 10 minutes

Data Files:

C:\084592Data\Getting Started with PowerPoint\Business Presentation.pptx

Scenario:

Your company, OGC Properties, has just purchased and installed the Microsoft Office suite. Because your job responsibilities typically require you to use PowerPoint to create presentations at business meetings, you decide to get to know the application.

---

1. Open the Business Presentation.pptx file from the C:\084592Data\Getting Started with PowerPoint folder.

---

2. Explore the Quick Access toolbar, Ribbon, and Backstage view.

---

3. Navigate and view the presentation using different views such as Normal, Slide Sorter, Reading, and Slide Show.

---

4. Save the file in the **PowerPoint 97–2003** file format with a different name and in a different location.

---

5. Explore the PowerPoint Help feature to find information on new features such as the Backstage view and file formats.

---

6. Close the presentation.

Lesson 2 Lab 1

Working with a Presentation

Activity Time: 10 minutes

Before You Begin:

The PowerPoint application is open.

Scenario:

You have just familiarized yourself with the basics of creating a PowerPoint presentation. You now wish to apply this knowledge to create a presentation for the Sales Team meeting.

1. Create a new blank presentation.

2. Apply the **Title and Content** slide layout to slide 1.

3. Enter the title as *Sales Team Meeting* in slide 1.

4. Insert a comparison slide as slide 2.

5. Insert a new slide as slide 3.

6. Change the layout of slide 3 to your choice.

7. Apply the **Concourse** theme to the presentation.

8. Move slide 3 before slide 2 using the Slide Sorter view.

9. Save the presentation as *My SalesTeam.pptx.*

10. Close the presentation.

Lesson 3 Lab 1

Applying Text Formatting to Slides

Activity Time: 10 minutes

Data Files:

C:\084592Data\Formatting Text on Slides\Organizational Goals.pptx

Scenario:

While reviewing a presentation, you find that the text in it is in the default format and visually unappealing. You want to apply the character and paragraph styles to enhance the visual appearance of text in the presentation.

1. Open the Organizational Goals.pptx file from the C:\084592Data\Formatting Text on Slides folder.

2. Apply bold formatting to the title text on slide 1.

3. Apply the colored underline style to all the slide titles after slide 1.

4. Apply a double-line spacing between the main bullet points on slide 3.

5. Apply a WordArt style of your choice to the title on slide 5.

6. Save the file as *My Organizational Goals.pptx.*

Lesson 4 Lab 1

Inserting Graphical Objects

Activity Time: 10 minutes

Data Files:

C:\084592Data\Adding Graphical Objects to a Presentation\OGC Business Data.pptx

Scenario:

You have created a financial overview presentation for your client. As the presentation is to be viewed by the upper management, you want to add some visual elements to the presentation to make it visually interesting.

1. Open the OGC Business Data.pptx file from the C:\084592Data\Adding Graphical Objects to a Presentation folder.

2. Insert the Businesses, Businessmen, and Charts clip art in slide 6.

3. On slide 5, apply a shape style of your choice to the rectangle shapes.

4. Apply a WordArt style of your choice to the existing title text on slide 1.

5. Save the presentation as *My OGC Business Data.pptx* and close it.

Lesson 5 Lab 1

Working with Graphical Objects

Activity Time: 10 minutes

Data Files:

C:\084592Data\Modifying Graphical Objects in Presentations\Annual Fundraiser.pptx

Scenario:

You are adding the final touches to your organization's annual charity fund-raiser presentation. There is a clip art on slide 6 that you want to use as a bullet icon. To do this, you need to proportionally reduce the size of the image so that it is not much taller than the height of the text in the list. Once you have the images in place as bullet icons, you will have to group them to preserve their alignment.

1. Open the Annual Fundraiser.pptx file from the C:\084592Data\Modifying Graphical Objects in Presentations folder.

2. Compress the file size of the clip art on slide 6.

3. Use the resized graphic as a bullet to number the first sentence.

4. Duplicate the image three times.

5. Move the duplicate image copies to the left of each of the remaining three list items.

6. Align and group the images.

Lesson 6 Lab 1

Inserting Tables

Activity Time: 10 minutes

Data Files:

C:\084592Data\Working with Tables\Annual Fundraiser.pptx, C:\084592Data\Working with Tables\Fundraiser Financials.doc

Scenario:

A representative from your company's Human Resources department has asked you to promote an annual charity fund-raiser at the next department meeting. You have taken some information that the representative sent you and used it to create a basic PowerPoint presentation. The representative wants you to incorporate additional information about last year's fund-raiser. This new information is sent to you in two tables. You are provided with a sheet of paper that contains information about organizations and the number of applicants served. Details are provided in the following table.

Organization	*Applicants Served*
Homeless Hostels	422
Mackenzie House	71
LCAA	233
CDPHP	312
Strike Out Hunger	749
Valiant Volunteers	695

The other table was sent to you as a Microsoft Word document named Fundraiser Financials.doc. You need to present the information contained in the Word document.

1. Open the Annual Fundraiser.pptx file from the C:\084592Data\Working with Tables folder.

2. Create a table with two columns and seven rows on slide 5.

3. Insert the data provided in the scenario into the table you created.

4. Modify the width of the columns to exactly fit the content.

5. Change the color of the header row.

6. Align the content in the right column to the center.

7. Import the table from the Fundraiser Financials.doc file to slide 10.

8. Save the file as **My Annual Fundraiser.pptx** and close it.

Lesson 7 Lab 1

Adding Charts to a Presentation

Activity Time: 10 minutes

Data Files:

C:\084592Data\Working with Charts\Annual Fundraiser.pptx, C:\084592Data\Working with Charts\Charity Distribution.xlsx, C:\084592Data\Working with Charts\FundraiserFinancials.docx

Before You Begin:

The Microsoft PowerPoint application is open.

Scenario:

While reviewing your presentation for a charity fundraiser, a coworker suggests that the data on slide 10 may be better presented as a chart rather than a table. After reviewing the slide, you agree that a chart might be an appropriate format. You decide to delete the table and use the information in the FundraiserFinancials.docx file to create a chart on slide 10 to present the Goal and Actual Donation data. Because the Percent Increase values are in a very different data range than the Goal and Actual Donation values, you decide to add a chart to slide 11 to display the Percent Increase data. Also, you want to paste a pie chart on slide 5 from an Excel spreadsheet file named Charity Distribution.xlsx.

1. Open the Annual Fundraiser.pptx file from the C:\084592Data\Working with Charts folder.

2. Create a column chart on slide 10 to represent the goal and actual donation data by using the information in the FundraiserFinancials.docx file.

3. Paste the chart from the Charity Distribution.xlsx spreadsheet file onto slide 5.

4. Save the presentation as **Annual Fundraiser.pptx** and close it.

Lesson 8 Lab 1
Finalizing a Presentation

Activity Time: 10 minutes

Data Files:

C:\084592Data\Preparing to Deliver a Presentation\Final Presentation.pptx

Before You Begin:
Open the Final Presentation.pptx file.

Scenario:
You have created a presentation and need to deliver it. You want to divide the presentation into two sections that deal with the main issues of your meeting. You also want to perform a spell check to ensure that it is error free and apply transition and animation effects. In addition to this, you want to create speaker notes to help you when delivering the presentation.

1. Open the Final Presentation.pptx file from the C:\084592Data\Preparing to Deliver a Presentation folder.

2. Run the spell checker and correct the spelling mistakes in the presentation.

3. Split the presentation into two sections and rename them as *Introduction* and *Financial Review,* respectively.

4. Apply the **Dissolve** transition effect to the entire presentation.

5. Add a speaker note to review the customer feedback on the Customer Expectations slide.

6. Change the default page size and print a copy of the presentation.

7. View the slide show.

8. Save the file as *My Final Presentation.pptx* and close it.

Glossary

Animation Painter
A feature that copies formatting from one place and applies it to another.

AutoCorrect dialog box
A dialog box that is used to control the AutoCorrect behavior.

AutoCorrect
A feature that is used to fix common typographical errors, and apply common formatting to characters thereby enhancing the value of your text.

background style
A color and texture that is applied to the background of the slide.

Backstage view
An interface that contains a series of tabs that group similar commands, and allows you to set the permissions, compatibility, and version information of the PowerPoint application.

border
The lines surrounding a cell in a table.

cells
The individual boxes inside a table where data is entered.

character formats
A set of built-in formatting options that would affect the size, color, and style when applied to text.

chart layouts
The predefined layout options for charts.

Chart pane
A pane that contains a sample chart plotted from data in an Excel worksheet.

chart styles
Predefined styles based on the chart type, chart layout, and presentation theme.

Chart Tools
A tool tab that includes commands that enable you to modify and enhance the design and layout of charts.

chart
A pictorial representation of numeric data stored in a table or spreadsheet.

Clear All Formatting
A button that removes all formatting applied to selected text.

Clip Art pane
A pane that is used to search for images to be used in a presentation.

clip art
A digital image that can be inserted into presentations.

columns
The vertical arrangement of cells in a table.

Compatibility Checker
A feature that enables you to identify the compatibility of objects used in presentations with the earlier versions of PowerPoint.

contextual tabs
The additional tabs containing specialized commands that are displayed by selecting specific object types such as tables, charts, or pictures.

data label
A label that labels the elements of a chart with their actual data values.

dialog box launchers
The small buttons with downward pointing arrows located at the bottom-right corner of certain command groups.

embedding
A method of inserting an external object in a slide. Embedded objects do not change when the source file is changed.

Format Painter
A feature that provides an easy way to copy only the formatting applied to text.

galleries
The libraries that list the varying outcomes of using certain commands on the Ribbon.

gradient effects
The mix of two or more colors to form a unique color and design pattern.

gridlines
The horizontal and vertical lines that crisscross each other, dividing the slide into square boxes of equal dimensions.

grouping
A technique in which multiple objects can be grouped together to form a single entity.

guides
The vertical and horizontal lines that are used to position objects on a slide.

handouts
The support material that can be used by the audience to make notes during a presentation.

image compression
A technique that reduces the file size of an image.

Landscape
A page orientation preferred to view the entire page on screen at once without wasted space along the sides.

legend
A box that helps you identify the colors that are assigned to each category in a chart.

linking
A method of inserting an external object in a slide. Linked objects are updated when the source file is changed.

Live Preview
A feature that enables you to view the formatting without actually applying them.

Mini toolbar
A floating toolbar that appears beside the selected text and consists of commonly used formatting options.

Normal view
The default view when a new presentation is created or an existing presentation is opened.

Notes Page view
A presentation view that displays a slide with its notes below it.

order of objects
A sequence that determines how overlapping objects appear on a slide.

orientation
The angle at which an image appears on a slide.

Outline tab
A tab that displays only the text of all the slides in a presentation.

outlines
The printed material that contains the slide title and text on each slide.

Paste Preview
A temporary live preview option that is available for different paste options.

Photo Album

A feature that enables you to insert and display photographs of your choice as a presentation.

Portrait

A page orientation option preferred where the height of the display area is greater than the width.

PowerPoint

An application that is part of the Microsoft Office suite used to create presentations.

presentation

An action of expressing an idea or a message to others.

Quick Access toolbar

A toolbar that provides easy access to the commonly used commands in the application.

Reading view

A presentation view that displays the presentation onscreen, one slide at a time within the window, similar to how it will be presented to an audience.

Research task pane

A pane that allows you to look up information by using online references.

Ribbon

A tabular component at the top of the user interface that provides quick access to task-specific commands.

rows

The horizontal arrangement of cells in a table.

Save As Template

A feature that saves a chart type as chart template.

scaling

The process of adjusting the size of an object proportionately.

ScreenTip

A small window that displays descriptive text upon pointing the mouse over a command, button, or control.

shapes

The simple geometric objects that can be modified to use as building blocks within a presentation.

slide layout

A slide template that determines the placement of content on a slide.

Slide Sorter view

A presentation view that displays all the slides as thumbnails.

Slides tab

A tab that displays a thumbnail of all the slides in a presentation.

slides

The presentation objects that display an idea.

speaker notes

Support material that can be printed for reference during a presentation.

Spell Checker

A feature that is used to check a presentation for spelling errors.

status bar

The bar that provides basic slide information and quick access to viewing options.

Switch rows/columns

A feature that enables you to swap data between the X and Y axis as desired

table styles

A combination of formatting options including color settings that can be applied to a table.

table

A container that consists of boxes called cells.

template

A layout that includes predefined elements such as backgrounds and color schemes.

text alignment

The position of text inside a text box.

text placeholder

A container that holds text in a slide.

texture

A characteristic of the appearance of a slide background.

theme

A combination of colors, fonts, and graphics that provides a consistent visual look and feel to a presentation.

Thesaurus

A reference tool that gives you a collection of synonyms and antonyms for a selected word.

thumbnails

The very small pictures of slides, about the size of your thumb.

title

A phrase that describes the data in a chart.

transitions

The special effects that appear while navigating through a slide show.

typography effects

The predefined formatting options that are applied to the text in a presentation.

ungrouping

An technique that allows the splitting of a grouped object into individual pieces.

WordArt styles

The predefined text effects that can be used to make text colorful and attractive.

WordArt

A text style that you can apply to text to turn it into a piece of art, which can be edited.

Index